99 Ways To Flood Your Website With Traffic

By: Mick Macro

Mick Macro

Text Copyright © 2014
REZZnet
All Rights Reserved

No right to redestribute, copy, amend or exploit materials. The information presented represents the view of the author at the date of publication and not the publisher, and by rate at which conditions change, the author reserves rights to update opinions based on new conditions. Neither author nor publisher assume any responsibility for errors or omissions. This book is in no way endorsed or distributed by any brand/company/site/etc. listed herin, are the sole opinions of the author, and should be treated as such.

99 Ways To Flood Your Website With Traffic

Preface

This book is all about flooding your website with traffic, and lists 99 tips, strategies, and techniques for getting lots of traffic to your websites, blogs, videos, and any type of online content.

Because there are 99 different strategies, the chapters in these books are shorter than most others out there. However, you can be assured that this book is packed with valuable content, and dives straight into the details and strategies, no fluff, no B.S.

Here are some of the things you'll learn in the book:

1. Lots of free sources of traffic
2. Some paid sources of traffic (only the cheapest and most targeted)
3. "Secret" sources of traffic that many don't know about
4. Direct step-by-step strategies
5. Tips for putting your website traffic on autopilot

And many more.

If you are having trouble with getting traffic to your website, blog, or other online content, your search stops here.

Every time you need to get some traffic flowing, just refer back to any of these strategies, take action, and reap the rewards of lots of visitors to your sites.

Note: You don't have to use all 99 strategies in order to get lots of visitors. There are some who rely on only a couple sources of traffic, and do very well. However, my only advice is to get your traffic from many different sources, so <u>when</u> one traffic source dies, your website doesn't die with it.

Hope you enjoy the book!

Talk to you soon.

Mick Macro

Free Sources of Traffic

The first half (more than half) of this book is all about free sources of traffic. However, when I say "free", you still may have little fees for setting up your website, an email list, hosting, domain name(s), etc.

I assume you already have a website or blog (or youtube channel, etc.). Most of these won't take ANY money to set up or implement, while some (like an email list) may take a small investment. So if you have $0 right now, don't worry, you'll be able to implement most of these - enough to get you hundreds of thousands of visitors if you work hard.

1
ADD "SHARE BARS/BUTTONS" TO YOUR SITE

You've seen them before. Almost every successful blogger I know uses them.

Share bars and share buttons are simply buttons, links, or images that allow your users to share the articles/videos/content you post on your websites and blogs.

Now, you can go two ways with this. First, if the sharing site is popular (like twitter, google+, facebook, etc.), you can usually find some sort of sharing button specifically for each site you want your content shared with.

This works well because you have control over the specific sites, but works not so well because of all the different HTML code you have to put together to get all the buttons to show up.

You can also go another route, and that is downloading/installing a plug-in to your site or blog that has a full array of sharing buttons from dozens of sites of your choosing. Of course, this can be done with a couple clicks if you are using WordPress as your blog platform and/or content management system.

Just download a popular sharing button plug-in, install it into your WordPress blog, edit some settings on what buttons to show, where to show the buttons, and other options like color and font choices, and then enable the plug-in.

Now when you upload an article, post, page, video, podcast, ANYTHING to your blog, there are now many options for you and your visitors to share your content with others.

The types of buttons and websites you want to share to will vary on the different niches for your blogs. You may want to share your articles on one blog with stumbleupon and digg, while you want to share a comedy blog with facebook and twitter only.

Mick Macro

Don't go crazy with these buttons. If you have too many (I've seen some websites with 30 - 40 buttons on every page), you risk having people skip over your buttons all together. Make things easy on your audience. Add the buttons to your few favorite sites (make sure they are heavily visited by the people who view your site or blog), put them on all of your pages and posts, and watch the sharing happen!

2
"Give away" Valuable Content

There are a few different ways of giving away free content that I'll mention in this book, but for now, we're talking about giving stuff away to your website visitors.

People love free stuff. Even more, people love free stuff that SHOULD be worth a lot of money!

Do you make beats? Give some away in a special download package! Do you write about technology? Write a tutorial guide! Blog about gardening? Write a short gardening report/book!

Then, post it on your site for FREE.

From here, you can now share your free content EVERYWHERE you can. Twitter, facebook, youtube, freebie sites, and more - you can use all of the strategies in this book to generate traffic to your freebie.

Also, make sure you allow people to share your content with anyone. Tell them to share it with friends, their list, facebook friends, etc.

Here's The Golden Rule: ALWAYS make sure you add a lot of value, and mention your website in your free content. Don't go overboard with self-promotion. Just mention it at the beginning and end of the content (and maybe somewhere in the middle). The more people that find your info valuable, the more sharing, which gives you tons of valuable traffic.

3

USE THE "TELL A FRIEND" / "EMAIL A FRIEND" SCRIPT

Again, if you have a WordPress blog, there are hundreds of plug-ins that place a button on all your posts that allow people to click it and immediately send the link of that post to a friend via email.

This works great for many reasons.

First, people who want to save a post for later reading can send the link to the post directly to themselves to view later!

Next, people who think their friend, family member, or online buddy will like the post, will send it their way.

This creates a viral effect, where the possibilities are endless. Add a nice CTA (call to action) near the email button, and tell your visitors to share this with friends.

Sometimes you can find "email a friend" features within share buttons / share bar plug-ins. Look around, find one you like (and one that works and is easy to use), and add it to your blog - let your visitors do the work for you. Then, when new visitors come in to your site, these "new guys" will do the same thing.

4
Send Articles To People With Email Lists

Every successful blogger and web site owner has an email list.

And, if you've been on as many lists as I've been on in the past, you know that most of them have trouble providing amazing content to their email list subscribers, and instead bombard them with the "next cool product to buy".

It's becoming more and more evident that email lists only work when you provide your subscribers with valuable content.

So, instead of having these email list owners search for great content to send to their list, you will send your content to them.

Of course you need to make sure your content brings tons of value, and relates to the email list(s) you will contact. It also has to be either interesting, shocking, mind-blowing, super-helpful. You get the idea.

Once you produce some valuable content on your site, send it to a few dozen people who have email lists. Express to them that you think this content can bring extra value to their subscribers, and also tell them that you aren't selling anything in your post (you are just looking for good traffic for now, not buyers).

The more email list holders/owners you send your content to, the greater the chance you have at one of them sending it to a list of 1,000, or 10,000, heck I've had a girl that had a list of 50,000 people that she sent one of my articles to.

5
VIRAL PDF FILES SUBMISSION

This is one of the greatest viral strategies online, however only if done correctly.

Here's how it works (it's really simple, so I'm just going to go through the step by step system with you):

1. Write an amazing, breakthrough, completely valuable book, report, guide, or piece of content that can be made into a PDF document.
2. Add your website link to the PDF, either at the top, the bottom, or both. You can also mention your website if needed somewhere in the book, and provide a link there as well.
3. Create the PDF document, PROTECT it (it's easy, just search how to protect your PDF so no one else can edit it/re-brand it), and test to make sure the links work correctly.
4. Finally, you post your PDF everywhere you can, and encourage others to send it to their friends. You can write at the very beginning of the PDF document/book "This ebook is free courtesy of mywebsitehere.com, send it and share it with anyone you want!".

The key to making this work is sending it to a lot of people, and then enticing them to send it to others. The more people that see it, the better chance you have at getting continued visitors to your website (or wherever you want to link to from your PDF).

Here's some tips on where to start when sending and sharing your PDF:

- Upload the PDF to your web hosting server. You could use FTP (file transfer protocol), or the file manager that comes with your hosting. If you need help, just ask your host's support team (if your hosting service doesn't have 24/7 support, leave them now).
- Get the link for your PDF (should look something like "http://website.com/pdfdoc.pdf"), you will use this link and post it everywhere.
- Post the link on your blog, on your website, send it to your email list, post

it on facebook, post it on twitter, post it to freebie sites, use other traffic sources from this book to get traffic to your PDF download.
- Post your PDF to file sharing, file hosting, free file type sites. The more you post to, the bigger chance of making each seed file go viral.

Create 10 PDFs (all 5 - 20 pages each), upload them to your website, share the link everywhere you can, entice others to share it as well, and post it to many file sharing sites.

The more PDFs, the more you share it, the better the content, the greater your success.

6

RSS Feed Aggregation and Submission

This strategy is mainly for blogs, but even if you don't have a blog, you should listen up.

RSS means "really simple syndication", and is used to publish frequently updated blog posts (that's just my simple definition).

Basically, you use an RSS feed button on your blog, and your visitors are able to subscribe to your RSS feed. Then, every time you add a new post to your blog, the visitor's "feed reader" will update with the new post, and they will be able to read it.

Most people at least know that much about RSS feeds, now on to some juicy stuff:

There are THOUSANDS of websites/services out there that ping, share, and publicize your RSS feed for your website. Think of it like submitting your website to a directory, but instead it's an RSS feed that consistently updates.

The trick is, send your RSS feed link (usually something like "http://mywebsite.com/feed") to hundreds of feed aggregators and feed submitters. Most of these services are free. Once you submit your RSS link, the more you post, and the more valuable your content, the more readers (and subscribers/visitors/buyers) you can potentially have.

7
CORRECTLY RE-DIRECT YOUR 404 ERROR PAGE

Okay, there are dozens of work-arounds to doing this, I'm going to share the one that MOST people will be able to implement (and if you find it's still too difficult, do a quick search and find the way you like most).

You may or may not know what a 404 error page is. Basically, when someone types in your main URL correctly (mywebsite.com) but the characters to the right of the main URL don't lead you to any specific page on your site (mywebsite.com/missspelled-page-thatduznt-exist), they are led to your 404 error page.

So for all your broken links (could be your fault or others), they will see something like "404 error, not found, the requested URL was not found on this server".

Most people who see this page hit the "back" button, and you lose that visitor completely!

So, you can EDIT your 404 error page, so that a custom page comes up (maybe with links to your email list, an opt-in form, or link to the homepage), OR you can set it so that it redirects straight to your homepage!

Here's how to do it:

First, ask your hosting company, "What is the easiest way to edit my 404 error page?". Some hosting companies can do the entire thing for you, but ALL will at least tell you how it is done.

If your hosting company can set this up for you, let them do it for you!

However, if you must do it on your own, get all the help you can from your hosting company. Depending on how your servers are set up by your host, you may need to access the .htaccess file, and/or the 404.html file (or 404.php, whichever is easier for your host).

I can't possibly tell you all the different work-arounds to this, it's different for everyone. What I can tell you is why this helps - When you re-direct your 404 error page to your home page (or some other page), anyone who wants to get to your site, but went through an expired or broken link, or didn't type in the name of the extended URL correctly, will get to your homepage, or any other page you specify, instead of seeing the same error page they've seen a million times before.

Then, instead of your visitors leaving when they see this page, they will see your homepage, and continue navigating your website or blog.

If this is too difficult, you can revisit this later. 404 error page redirecting isn't the biggest traffic generator, anyway.

8

COMMENT ON POPULAR BLOGS

This strategy is great, as long as you continue to implement it every day (or at least every week).

Commenting on blogs does 2 AMAZING things for your website:

#1: It brings new human visitors from these blogs to your website directly (assuming you comment on blogs that allow your name to be linked to your website).

#2: If the links are "dofollow" (just do a search for "blogs:dofollow"), your site that you link to will begin to rise in popularity, and will show up more in the search engines, giving you even more visitors.

But again, most people hear about this, then they go comment on 20 random blog posts, and within a few hours, they see no results, and believe it just "doesn't work".

The more effort you put into this, the great the success (like anything). Let me give you a few tips on how to implement this strategy to the fullest:

- Always write long, valuable comments. These go a long way, and more people notice them. Always try to add to the content you are commenting on, give more knowledge on the topic.
- Never directly promote your website. Just link to it with your name (almost all blogs allow this). Then when someone finds your comment really inspiring or helpful, they'll click your name to find out more about you!
- Comment on HIGH PageRanked blogs. You don't have to look at the "Google PR" directly, just make sure you are commenting on blogs that are popular and that many others comment on.
- As long as you continue to write long, valuable comments, you should write up to 50 - 100 comments a day. The more you get your little blurbs

of knowledge and helpfulness (and links!) out there, the more visitors you will have.

Golden Rule: Don't just do this once. Keep up your blog commenting every single day, and you'll see your visitors build consistently.

9

Guest Post On Other Blogs

Guest posting can be a little time consuming, but it really does work wonders.

If you are able to write great, valuable content, most blogs (unless they already have a team of hired writers) will be HAPPY to post your articles to their website.

Here's how guest posting works:

First, make a list of blogs related to your blog or site, especially if you already know they accept guest post submissions. You can also find lots of "guest post enabled blog" directories/search engines, where blog owners are looking for your content.

Next, do some research on what type of articles are posted on these blogs. You don't want to copy their writing style exactly, but by having similar views, similar writing styles, and similar layouts makes it much easier for these bloggers to accept your submissions. Write a few articles, I'd say have a good list of 5 or 10.

Now this is the part that is a little time consuming...

You obviously can't send the same article to 10 or 20 blogs, because you would soon be labeled a scammer, as it's looked down upon to have duplicate content on your blog.

This is why it's good to write 10 or 20 articles over the course of a few hours (keep each article on one topic only), and send each one to ONLY ONE specific blogger.

Here's how to speed up the process:

Mick Macro

- Express to the person you send your article to that you would love for them to post it on their site, and all you need in return is a link to your website at the bottom of the post.

- Put a time limit on a response! Now, you don't need to put a time limit on when they need to post the article, but you want to let them know you need a response within a few days, so you at least let you know they are going to post it.

This way, if you don't get a response within your set time limit, you can then try sending that article to another blog author.

10
INVITE OTHERS TO GUEST POST ON YOUR BLOG

You got it, guest posting works to your advantage both ways.

By inviting others to guest post on your blog, you have three direct advantages:

1. There's no true work on your end. You may have to choose a title and add a picture, but all the content is already there! Once you get a submission, choose whether or not it fits on your blog/website, post it, and you're done! This process can take as little as 5 minutes.
2. More content = More visitors. Besides not having to do any work, you'll get plenty of visitors from search engines (and other traffic sources). Just use the promotion tactics from this book for these blog posts - isn't it great getting visitors for work you didn't do?
3. The author of the post may link to the article. Usually when someone is guest posting on someone else's blog, once it is published and live, they want to tell everyone they know about it! This works great for you, because the more guest posts you have, the greater the chance at thousands (and more) of people visiting your blog. Sometimes you'll get bloggers, authors, info product creators, and writers emailing their entire list of thousands, and sharing the article everywhere they can.

Here's how to get people to post on your blog:

First, set up a page on your site/blog, and call it something like "Guest Posting", "Guest Bloggers", "Write For This Blog", "Bloggers Needed" - or something like that.

On this page, tell people that you are giving them the opportunity to write for your blog as a guest blogger. Don't say "please write for my blog", instead say "I'm allowing you to write for my blog".

Give them clear specifications as to what type of posts you will accept. Make sure they understand completely what you expect, otherwise you'll get hundreds of worthless posts that you would never post to your blog (and therefore wastes time).

Finally, make a new email address specifically for article submissions. Post the email address to this page, or better yet, make a "contact form" that allows file uploads/sending.

One more thing: Make sure you express that you are going to give them credit for each article submitted, and can provide a link to their website/blog/twitter/etc. at the bottom of the post (or in the author resource box if you have one set up).

Go ahead, take the 1 hour (or less) to set this page up, and check your new email every few days, or whenever you want. You'll soon have lots of submissions rolling in, especially if you use a lot of the other tactics in this book to generate traffic to your guest post page.

11
ONE WAY BACKLINKS

Now, this "strategy" really covers a lot of things, but I really think it's important enough to mention it in it's entirety.

One way backlinks are simply external links that point back to your website or blog, without you having to link back to their site in return (this would be called a "link exchange").

Now, of course you can post your website URL to twitter or facebook, and that would technically be a link - but, if you really want to up your link juice, you must venture outside of the norms.

There's plenty of sites out there that would be happy to have a link on their site pointing to your website. Why?

Well, simply because most of the time, you can do it yourself. There are a lot of strategies for link building in this book that you can implement and get results immediately.

Others may take some more time, but are more worth it because of the heightened results they bring. For instance, MILLIONS of people are posting on twitter every day. Your link will be lost in the action pretty soon. But nail a link on another niche website related to yours with a high page rank and a lot of visitors, and you'll find that search engines LOVE links like this.

Backlink Scams To Stay Away From:

Now, these can help a little with link juice, but for the most part aren't worth a second of your time.

If a website tells you they can get you 10,000 backlinks for free, then you know it's definitely an automated process, and anyone else can post their links here.

Mick Macro

Most people will tell you sites and services like this could hurt your rankings in search engines. Two words: I agree.

You would be better off finding a good website with high page rank to exchange links with, as you'll learn about in this next chapter.

12
Link Exchanges

Yeah yeah yeah, everyone knows about link exchanges, right?

Most people will skip this chapter, thinking they know everything there is to know about exchanging links - however, they're probably not doing it the right way.

In the old world of the internet, you could simply have a "link list page" full of thousands of links, and exchange links with any site willing and able. Search engines then saw the huge amount of links pointing to your site, and rank you better.

Now to the new age:

Search engines are penalizing more and more websites because of low quality sites (I'm talkin' SUPER low quality) linking to your website.

Most people do link exchanges this way. Add another site to the list of links, and have your site added to their list of links. You will do things differently. Instead, do a "full page" or "full article" exchange.

Here's why this works better for both parties: Both links will essentially be the ONLY links on this specific page or article, which brings more link juice, and doesn't look spammy to search engines, it just looks like another page they should index and rank.

You may think this is difficult to do, but let me tell you that it's not hard at all. These pages don't have to be spectacular. Exchange images for the page/post, a description/content (can be really short), and the link to post. Only takes a few minutes, and you have prominent links on fellow websites.

One more thing to think about when exchanging links is the relevancy of the website to your own. Take a brief look at the keywords, titles, and content of the site. Does it relate to your website? Would you like to be ranked and indexed for keywords like this? Because you better believe if you get 100 sites about "dog training" linking to you, search engines will start to believe your website is indeed related to dog training!

Remember, a lot of links are great, but it's better to focus on a small handful of high quality sites to exchange links with.

13

TORRENT SITES

This is something too many people are still missing out on.

Torrent uploading is so simple, I'm surprised that more people don't do it. Let me break this strategy down into steps for you, then I'll go ahead and explain it in further detail.

1. Make some great content. Make sure the final piece of content is either a PDF file, or an AUDIO file, or any other type of file you can convert to a torrent file. I'm going to use PDFs and .mp3 files for this example strategy.
2. Convert your file to a torrent file. This is simple, just convert your content into a torrent for easy uploading to torrent websites.
3. Post your torrent file to torrent sharing sites. Post it to 5, post it to 100, the more the better.

Okay, now on to the major details of this strategy:

When you are creating your content, make sure you mention your website. If it's a PDF, add a link to your website as many times as you want. If it's an audio file, make sure there is some sort of tag or promotion that says this content is from your website.

Another tip is to name your file something that people are going to be interested in. If it's a PDF titled "How To Use Facebook Advertising", you can leave that as the title inside the PDF, but name the file something like "How To Absolutely CRUSH IT With Cheap Facebook Ads". More people will download files with enhanced titles like this.

The key is continuing to create a gigantic arsenal of free content made into torrent files (you can see a list of 1,000s of files one day), and then continue your efforts by uploading ALL of the files to 100s of torrent sites.

10 files X 1,000 downloads each = 10,000 people seeing a link or promotion for your

Mick Macro

website.

1,000 files x 10,000 downloads each = 10,000,000 people seeing a link or promotion for your website.

Yes, it sounds crazy to even think of these numbers. Don't think you are crazy - this is possible. You just have to take action, create great content, submit your content EVERYWHERE, and continue your efforts all the time.

14
Ping All The Time

This chapter is going to be short, but again, it's a vital part of your traffic generation strategy.

Pinging is used to tell search engines (and basically the world) that your website or page or post exists. And if they already knew it existed, it will still update a new ping with all of the new content you've added to your website or blog.

Just search "ping sites" or "ping my site", you'll find tons of websites that can ping your site to TONS of search engines and directories.

If you've never pinged your website(s) before, DO IT NOW. Ping every page, every post, especially the home page!

If you have used pinging before, that's great. Do you use it on every new article you post? Do you ping your site every time you update it? If not, you can, and it brings great results. By continuously pinging your website every time it is updated (like a new blog post), search engines and ping websites will recognize that your site is changing all the time, which search engines love.

Bottom line: Ping every piece of new content on your website. If you use a free service that pings your site to multiple search engines, then it takes 5 seconds or less to ping. COPY URL + PASTE URL + PING!

15
SEARCH ENGINE SUBMISSION

Many confuse search engine submission with pinging.

I'm not going to get into every technical detail of why you need to do both, but put simply: they are completely different things, different services, different paramaters, different "directories" of submissions.

One of the main differences is that once your site is indexed in a certain search engine, it's pointless to submit again since it would be put in the same place - it doesn't add any juice or extra link somewhere.

- For many search engines, you can go directly to one of their pages to submit your site to each search engine for free (some also have paid inclusion, in which your site is indexed immediately).

- Then you have the free search engine submission sites/services. These guys will submit your site to a set amount of search engines (usually between 20 - 100) for no cost whatsoever.

- Finally, you have paid search engine submission sites/services. These services usually submit your site to many more search engines than the free services, and usually guarantees inclusion or some other type of added value.

If you have the money, go for the paid options - your site will be indexed quicker than you've ever seen before. If you don't have the money, no problem! You can use the free services, and still get your site at least looked at or spidered by search engines.

16
REVIEW OTHER CONTENT, AND LINK TO IT

Now, this is similar to "content curation", but there's a better way of doing curation besides just posting a link to a "cool article".

When you find an article, a video, a tutorial, a page on a website with great info, share it on your blog.

This isn't as "push-button simple" as you think it is. In fact, you might still be wondering how this is going to help you get visitors to your website.

Don't just post a link to someone's article with the words "hey click here to check this out". Instead, add more to what you are linking to. Tell your audience how great the article/content is, link to it, and then add your own added value below the link.

For you bloggers, it's easiest to do it this way: No matter what content you are linking to (podcast, article, video, etc.), just add a paragraph or two (more or less) of content.

Okay, here's how it helps YOU:

After you write about someone's content and publish the article (make sure you include a link to their site/content), TELL THEM ABOUT IT.

Send them an email, @mention their twitter account, leave a comment or two on some of their recent posts (or better yet, the post you linked to!). Get YOUR post in front of THEIR eyes - it's easiest if you mention the blogger's name in the title.

Once they see that you've written a post that...

    a. Is all about them

and

b. Has added extra value,

most will be happy to link to you, or update their own article to include a link to your article. Maybe they'll tell people about your content. Maybe they'll mention you on twitter. The point is, the more you do this, and the better your extra added value, the better your chances at these bloggers mentioning you in the future, as well as checking out your blog from time to time.

Reviewing and adding value to content can be a good way to gain relationships with other bloggers, and bring more of a community to your own blog. However, if this doesn't sound fun at all to you, don't even worry about it, because there are other quicker traffic strategies.

17
Free Promotion / Link Sites

"Submit your link here!", "Add your site", "Submit URL", you've seen these types of sites before.

They offer the service of posting a link to your site for free. As I've said before, you should watch out for a lot of these. Some of these free link sites will simply post your link to poor quality sites.

Just search for "submit url", "add your site", and "submit website", and you'll find tons of sites that are able to post your link to their site (or lists/directories of sites).

The only thing I'll mention before continuing with this strategy is don't expect a whole lot. Yes, these types of free link sites can help, but often times you won't notice a direct increase in visitors.

So, don't look at this strategy as a direct strategy for getting visitors. It's more about link building.

For instance, I used to own a music site that was getting around 1,000 visitors per day. Then, I started submitting my site to link sites and promo sites for free. After posting to a dozen sites within an hour, I checked back to see my traffic. Although there wasn't a huge increase, I noticed a few visitors from the various sites.

Then, for the next week, I submitted my site to around 200 sites total - and although I only saw a small increase in visitors, that increase continued slowly over time, and I began to get more and more visitors.

I also noticed in sites like "Alexa", or any traffic/ranking site, I was ranking better, had many more backlinks, and my website LOOKED much better to future visitors and stat checkers.

Mick Macro

Don't make this your only traffic strategy. Spend an hour on this every once and awhile, then move on. Continue to implement other link building and traffic strategies on top of this, and just make this one more piece of the puzzle.

18

START USING LONG-TAIL KEYWORDS

This is one strategy that has been around for many years, and it will continue to work for as long as search engines still exist.

Your blog and/or website has thousands of keywords on it. The more a keyword shows up, the more search engines look at that specific keyword. Search engines take your most used/prominent keywords on your site, and rank you for them. Then it's a whole big combination of how well your content is, the competition for the keyword, how many links you have coming into your site, social media sharing, and many more.

Some of these keywords will be core keywords, like "weight loss" and "fishing". Longer-tail keywords would be "How To Lose 10 Pounds In 5 Days" and "How To Properly Gut A Fish". These long tail keywords are much easier to rank for, as you most definitely have a lot less competition for these. Then you can get into super-long-tail keywords, like "The Greatest 100 Flash Mobs Of The Entire Flash Mob History".

One thing you need to think about however… is that the more long-tail you go, the less competition, but also the less people searching for that long keyword phrase. So you CAN write an article titled "The Greatest 100 Flash Mobs Of The Entire Flash Mob History", but you'll find out that it may only get 1 or 2 exact match searches every month.

So, you must find a happy medium. I would say to first experiment on your own with some different keyword phrases, and find your own happy medium. Then, go for some long-tails, and some short-tails, work them all in to enhance your search result rankings, and therefore your traffic.

Another great way to find good keywords is The Google Keyword Tool. Just search it in Google, it will most likely be the first search result.

Mick Macro

With the Google Keyword Tool, you are able to enter in as many keywords as you want, and get keyword ideas, the competition of the keywords, and how many searches there are for that keyword each month. Make sure you hit the "exact match" check box to see the competition and searches for the entire exact keyphrase, as it will give you more realistic numbers on how many actual searches there are for an entire keyword phrase.

If you are already getting traffic, long-tail keywords are great because you can usually rank high for those keywords pretty quickly. And if you still are struggling with traffic, long-tail keywords are your "in". Start with the long-tail, get some visitors from search engines, and then go shorter. Keep going back and forth, find your happy medium, and continue your efforts for lots more traffic.

19
Squidoo and Sharing

Okay, these next two strategies are ones I use just about everyday - really whenever I post new content to my blogs, I'll post something to sites like these.

The best part is, with the growing internet, if these 2 websites (or any other site mentioned in this book) don't exist one day, there will always be an alternative - ALWAYS - trust me.

So, let's talk about Squidoo.

Squidoo is a site that allows you to post "lenses", which are just pages of content, and add "modules", which can consist of text, video, audio, images, links (to your website), and more.

Besides getting visitors, you can actually make money from the content you post to Squidoo. Make money from ads, post modules for physical products and make a commission from them, and more. You can go join Squidoo and check out all the monetization methods they have, but I'm going to dive more into traffic generation from Squidoo.

Think of Squidoo like this: If you were to post a piece of content on your own website, you are relying on your own stats, ranking, and visitors for that content to become popular. If you have minimum visitors, low site rank, and not a lot of content, you're going to have to do a lot of extra promotion for the article to gain any exposure. Post that same content to Squidoo, on a site that is most likely MUCH more popular than yours, with their own visitors, high site page rank, and extra promotion (squid likes as it's called now), just from posting your content on Squidoo and other sites like this.

Now, onto getting these visitors to YOUR website:

Post a link to your website once or twice in the lens. If there is a helpful article on your site that relates to this lens, post a link to that as well! Write great content, add lots of value to people's lives, and you will be rewarded with new visitors to your site every day.

If you've used sites like these, and haven't gotten results, it's because you are missing one key aspect: you must first get your lens popular before the lens makes your site popular.

Use all of the "sharing" buttons on your lens to share it with the world! Tweet it, share it on facebook, "squid like" it, entice others to share this FREE CONTENT around with others.

And one more piece of advice: If you really want to pump thousands of visitors to your website from Squidoo, give away something on your website for free. Mention it a few times in your Squidoo lens (as long as it relates to the topic you are writing about). Most of these people would LOVE to have a free book, free report, free audio, video, etc.

You can give them a direct download on the lens, or direct them to your website where your free download is posted, OR have them opt-in to your email list in order to get your free content (more on that later).

Anything you can do to entice others to visit your blog/site, DO IT. But above and beyond anything else, it all comes down to the value of your content. Post great content, do a little promotion, and you'll have visitors all day long.

20
HubPages and Sharing

HubPages is sort of like Squidoo. I'd say Squidoo has a lot more options, and in my mind is going to be around for decades (as long as the internet exists I'd hope).

However, it's important to know that there are sites like HubPages, and thousands like it, that give you the same sort of options of posting your own content on their site/hub.

You will tend to notice that some people like Squidoo, others like HubPages, and some even like those other sites that hardly get any visitors. It's all up to the preference of each person online. So, in order to get the most bang for your buck, I would say it's best to not put all your eggs in one basket, and start posting content to many content hubs online.

HubPages has a clean, simple look. They have the same sort of sharing options available. You can publish a "hub", share it around, and get it ranking WAY faster than you could if you posted the content on your own site.

In a month, if you posted 100 articles to a handful of 4 or 5 sites like this, and all content valuable content, you can expect hundreds and thousands of new visitors to your site every day.

It's all about quantity + quantity. Most say go for one or the other, I say do both. Get lots of content out there, and make it as good as you can. You don't have to reinvent the wheel and post 5,000 word lenses expecting more visitors - instead get a dozen 400 word lenses published, with great topic-specific content, and link to your website and tell them "if you want more great stuff like this, click here and visit my blog/site".

21
BLOGGER BLOGS / FREE BLOG SITES

This strategy works like the content hub strategies above, however differ in a few ways.

With the Squidoo/HubPages style of getting visitors, you are able to post content on these sites, without you having to actually "own" a site or space online.

With this "free blog sites" strategy, you are instead signing up for and publishing dozens of blogs (for free) - some one WordPress, some on Blogger, as well as other free blogging sites in existence (again, there are THOUSANDS).

By now, you should already know the importance of having your own domain name. So instead of CoolestSiteForRagDollMaking.WordPress.com, you have CoolestSiteForRagDollMaking.com - see the difference?

If you want your own domain name, it costs money. I would suggest that for your main blog or site, you should absolutely 100% buy your own domain.

However, for this strategy, you will create dozens of "micro-sites" or "super-niche-sites" as I like to call them, and you will publish them for free right on these blogging platforms.

If your site is called "BestBreakdancingTutorials.com", you could make a list of niche sites like:

- bestbreakdancingtutorialsever.wordpress.com

- breakdancingfordummies.wordpress.com

- the-breakdancing-site.blogger.com

99 Ways To Flood Your Website With Traffic

- bboys-and-bgirls.blogger.com

- superdancevideos.wordpress.com

You get the picture. Set up these sites, add some content (don't go crazy, just a few articles will do for now), and link to your main website from all of these sites.

Then, from time to time, post an article, or embed someone else's YouTube video to these blogs, and continue to post links to your main site(s).

This does so many great things for your website. It gives you LOTS of incoming back links, brings in lots of direct visitors that view these niche blogs/sites, and also brings you higher site rankings and more search engine traffic.

The more blogs you create, and the better each one is, the more traffic you could essentially bring to your website.

22
Ask/Answer Sites

People have questions, and people want answers!

That's where sites like Yahoo Answers and Ask.com come into play. Sites like these allow people to post questions, and allow others to answer these questions right on the site.

Most of these sites also allow users to post "sources" in their answer. This means if someone wants to know how to purify water, someone can provide an answer, and then provide a link to a website saying "this is where I found some of this info".

These sites are getting smarter every day.

Now you have "answer rankings", and "levels", and a whole bunch of other stuff that basically says "this person usually has really good answers to questions."

So, here's what you need to do in order to get a lot of traffic from ask/answer sites:

- First, join about 5 or more of these websites.

- Then, search for questions in your niche/topic area.

- Find questions that relate to your website (or that your website has information about).

- Answer these questions thoroughly, and post a link to one of your articles that could "help them out further".

You don't even have to say it's YOUR site. Just say "I found this website helpful". And one note: Instead of posting a link to your website EVERY single time, try including links to other websites, to avoid the communities on these answer sites calling you a link spammer.

99 Ways To Flood Your Website With Traffic

The point is, if you respond to a question with a valuable answer, and people pick your answer as the best one, it goes a long way. So add value, answer the question in full detail, do this from time to time consistently, and you'll have more traffic each time you answer a question.

One more thing to note: This traffic does come instantly and quick, but is also residual traffic. Because now when someone types into a search engine "how to.... --question you've answered here--", that question will come up in the search results with an ANSWER. And when someone reads your answer, and it actually helps them, they'll be happy to find out more about you and your website.

23

Audio and Podcasting

Like other types of media, there are websites and services that LOVE to promote audio and podcasts!

Okay, here's how it works:

Podcasts are EASY to make. Simply find a topic (like you would if you were going to write a blog post), write a couple of key points that you want to talk about, and make the podcast! Also make sure you vocalize your website name (important!).

Most computers come equipped with microphone and recording ability. If so, use your computer mic and your favorite audio editing program (for starters, Mac users use Garageband, and PC users use Audacity - although this could change) to make the audio. Then export it to mp3.

If you have a nice microphone, that works even better! If you have neither, use a video camera, or camera phone, to record a simple video (you won't use the video). Once you are finished, use a "video to audio" conversion website to convert your video into an audio file.

Once you have the audio file, it's time to publish your podcast. If you use Wordpress, you can upload this directly to your account in "media". Or, you could also just upload your file to your file manager or via FTP - whatever your blog/site/hosting company uses.

Your URL for your podcast should look something like this: http://website.com/podcast1.mp3 OR http://website.com/podcastfolder/podcast1.mp3 if you make a folder called "podcastfolder".

Now comes publishing and promoting your podcast:

I find it best if you find a nice "plugin" on WordPress (or even just for any static site) that has an audio player, and it's even better if the plug-in is made specifically for podcasts (do your research). If you don't have access to, or don't want a plug-in, search for "html code audio player", and use the instructions to get your audio published!

Once your podcast is published, it's time to promote it.

First, use iTunes to publish your podcast there. Millions of people LOVE free podcasts. And since your website name is in the podcast (you DID mention your website, right?), you'll get a nice flow of visitors right from iTunes to your website.

Once it's on iTunes (the 8 million pound gorilla haha), it's time to promote your podcast in other places. Search for "podcast directory", "podcast promotion", "podcast submission", and other similar keywords.

There are thousands of sites that want to promote your podcast - take advantage of them. Post it to as many sites as you can. Most of these directories/promotion/submission platforms allow you to post a link to your website as well, so in the process of getting people listening to your podcast (and then visiting your website after), you will also get people just clicking on your website.

As you can see, the more media types you implement in your website, the more people you have access to. Jane might love listening to podcasts. Frank only likes long books. Billy likes short blog posts. Karen likes videos. If you have them all, you have that much more access to people, therefore bringing you more visitors.

24

Use the Facebook Comment Plugin

Ahhh yes, one of those things you see all over the place, but you probably haven't used, yet.

This is more for blogs only, but if you have a website or other type of site that has a comment section, you can very well use this too.

Long story short: Boring comment sections are boring. Spice it up with Facebook Comments!

No matter what blog platform you use, you can install facebook comments - However, I would recommend that you use Wordpress (it just makes your and everyone else's life easier).

Instead of going into all the details about installing the plugin or getting facebook comments on your blog (since it's super easy to install, and this aint no installation guide!), I'm going to tell you why this is so effective and brings a huge community to your blog.

I think it's easiest if I show you examples of how each type of comment system works:

Regular Boring Comment System:

- People find your blog, and start reading one of your posts.
- Maybe half of these visitors (or less) will get to the end of your post and see the comment section.
- Everyone will see it is a basic comment plugin, with no true interaction.

- Heck, most can't even display an avatar or picture, and some won't allow links in the comments.

- A very small percentage will comment. This will be small because there is no interaction besides them leaving a comment and then leaving your site.

- And... the comment stops here.

Facebook Comment Plugin System:

- People find your blog, and start reading one of your posts.

- Again, half of the visitors get to the end of the post and see your facebook comment section.

- When people see "facebook", they think "friends, interaction, talking, communicating, sharing". They see pictures, "likes", replies, and they are already used to commenting on facebook, so it makes it easy for them.

- You now get a higher percentage of people commenting. People are able to comment on your post, interact with you, get responses from others, and feel more inclined to come back.

- And... the comment DOES NOT STOP HERE.

- Some facebook comment plugins do this automatically, others give the visitor the option - When someone comments on your blog using the facebook comment plugin, a status update is posted to their facebook wall, for all their friends to see! If this person has 500 friends, that means 500 people now have access to your blog post. And if those 500 people comment, you could have virtually thousands, even millions of potential visitors.

Do you see the viral effect these types of traffic generation tactics have? Let others do the work for you!

25
SHARE ON TWITTER AND GAIN A COMMUNITY

Most people use twitter the wrong way.

Sure, most people who want to get traffic to their website have a twitter account. Heck, lots of people have 2 accounts! Few have even more than that.

However, most people use their twitter accounts the wrong way. They sign up for twitter, put their "follow me" button or link on their website, and then post links to their website non-stop on their twitter account.

Here's how to use Twitter the RIGHT way:

First of all, it's all about SHARING on twitter. You've got to gain a community of followers if you are ever going to get anywhere. The best way to get followers is by interacting with people on twitter.

Reply to someone's tweet. Follow tons of people. Guess what? The message feature is there for a reason, MESSAGE someone!

Next, you've got to get your follower count up. It's been proven by many people that the more followers you have, the easier it is to continually get more followers. It's like the saying goes, "the rich get richer and the poor well... are still poor" - it goes something like that ;)

Follow dozens of relevant twitter accounts every day (hundreds if possible). Find people that talk about the same thing as you (that's what the search feature is for). Tweet these people, message them, follow them.

Then, go to sites like twiends or other "get followers" or "follower exchange" sites. You can follow 100 people in 5 minutes, and have 100 new followers 10 minutes later. I've used this strategy of following 500 people, waiting a day for my followers to roll in, then I unfollow people (100 at a time so twitter doesn't hate me) until my "following" number is low, then I go back and follow more people using sites like this.

On top of that, you must provide valuable content. Don't spam your links all day. Post some inspiring quotes, post links to free stuff, fun videos, great articles, and occasionally one of your own promos - later on when your follower number increases to the thousands, you can start promoting offers and make money right away!

26
Facebook Pages and Timelines

Yes, facebook changes all the time. Instead of bitching and moaning about the change, it's time to keep up with the change.

First of all - timelines. You should have timeline enabled (I still see old ugly facebook accounts/walls). You should also be constantly publishing and promoting your content on your timeline.

Next is friends. Sure, we may not really have 5,000 friends in "real life", but heck, if these 5,000 friends are all people who would love to see the next piece of content you post, then add as many friends as you can.

It's easiest to friend request people who have more than 1,000 friends, so start there. Then, find others on facebook interested in the same stuff you are. Add them as a friend as well.

Keep building up your friends. If you get to the maximum amount, get rid of the "friends" that don't contribute much, and add new ones.

Okay, now about Facebook pages. You absolutely must have a facebook page for your website. I'd even have another facebook page for your personal life/friends. That way, if you hate deleting friends, you can forward them to your page which can have literally millions of "fans".

Did you know you can "use facebook as your page/website"? Yep, then you can scroll around facebook, finding people talking about things that you write about/post/do, and then you can provide them with your link to your website.

And besides your own pages, go search for other pages related to yours. There are so many facebook pages out there that allow the public to post content. And some of

99 Ways To Flood Your Website With Traffic

these pages have over 100,000 likes/fans! Post your link/article/freebie etc. to these pages, and your link could be in front of millions of eyes.

Don't underestimate the power of Facebook. Make more friends, get more likes, add valuable content, promote like crazy, and think outside the box.

27

POSTING YOUTUBE VIDEOS

If you haven't started making YouTube videos, you need to start doing so immediately.

YouTube has been around for too many years now, you must start a YouTube channel today. Since Google owns YouTube, you can bet that it's going to be around forever (so we hope), and there is only going to be more people watching videos in the future, and those people could be watching your videos instead of some other guy's.

I could write an entire book just on YouTube traffic, so I'm going to list my top strategies for getting traffic from YouTube:

- Don't make videos purely for just views. Focus on a clear CTA (call to action) at the end/start/middle of all your videos. What do you want them to do? Visit your website! So instead of telling them to subscribe or comment on your video, tell them to go check out your "newest cool thing" on your website.

- Give stuff away for free. Make a video telling people about the free stuff you are giving away. Whether it is a book, a free report, a piece of music, or any other free piece of content, go ahead and put it on your website, then make a video about it, and link to your website page where the freebie is. Put it this way: Make a useless video with no CTA, and get 1,000 video views and 0 website views. Make a nice video with a CTA, and get 1,000 video views and maybe 10 - 50 website views. Make a great video with multiple clear CTAs, AND give away a freebie, and you can expect even more views, and up to a 10% - 50%+ click through rate to your website.

- Always make sure there is a link to your website (even if it's to a blog post/freebie/etc.) at the TOP of the description. People can see the beginning of the description in search results, and when someone shares your video. Make use of this. Sometimes people don't even watch my video, and go ahead and click on my website link. Sure I don't get a video view, but I just got a website visitor, possibly multiple pageviews on my website, and quite possibly a return visitor.

- KISS (Keep It Simple, Stupid!) - You don't need to have the most amazing quality in the world. You don't need fancy equipment. You don't need special editing tricks, or even talking oranges! You can get more website visitors than any other person on YouTube just by creating clear CTAs, linking your website, and always encouraging people to continue the discussion and FUN on your website.

One more tip: If you are scared to get in front of the camera, don't worry. You can do a slideshow, or powerpoint style presentation, just text on the video, or even an audio recording with an image of your website. The possibilities are endless. Just get out there, make great content, subscribe to others, comment on other videos, and don't worry about the video views. There are people getting over 1 million video views, and only getting 100 website views out of that traffic. Then there are people who get a mediocre 1,000 - 5,000 video views, and get almost the same amount of website pageviews from this traffic. Sure, there may be only 500 people who came to the website. But when they visit a page or two (or 10!), all of those website page views start to add up.

28

TAKE ADVANTAGE OF OTHER VIDEO SHARING SITES

This should be a continuation of posting YouTube videos - all should coexist in your traffic plan.

Do you know about any other video sharing sites out there? Maybe a few? There's hundreds of popular ones, and thousands more on top of that. If you want to get more traffic, and you post videos to YouTube telling people to visit your website, why would you NOT post your video to other video websites?

Yes, to start, it might take a few hours to get dozens of video accounts set up. You'll probably also want to add your website link to your profile for starters.

But once all your video accounts are set up, you can make a video, and instead of publishing it just to YouTube, publish it on every single video account you have set up.

Tip: Use a browser that allows tabs. Then, open all the video sites in separate tabs. Log-in to all. Publish each video one at a time, and have a description with your website link handy to copy+paste in each description/info box. Once you've submitted to all the sites, wait until they are all processed and uploaded, and then sit back and enjoy.

You can post your video to 20 or 30 sites in the matter of 30 minutes (or longer if you have HD or very large files). Of course this brings direct visitors to your website, but it also does something else. By having 20, 30, 100+ video sharing sites linking to YOUR website, you better believe the search engines will start to take notice. Remember what I said earlier, keep focused on building links to ensure residual traffic each day.

And if you think this will take too long - there are websites and services that make things easier.

99 Ways To Flood Your Website With Traffic

I won't name a bunch of companies, because these tend to come and go quickly at times, but just search around for "video distribution", "post video to multiple video sites", and similar searches like that. You will find dozens of great companies that will tie in all of your login info to tons of different video sharing sites, and then allow you to upload your video through their server ONCE, then their server takes care of uploading the video, writing your title, tags, and description, and any types of links you want. Some of these services cost money, others are free. The free ones are great if you have no budget at all. However, the paid services in this area are always better as they are able to publish your video to more sites, post multiple videos at the same time, post your video to quality video sites that some other automated services don't have access to, and other goodies.

The point is, if you are posting videos to YouTube, you need to start posting them to other sites. There's other people out there that love other websites, and don't go on YouTube for certain reasons (maybe it's too many ads, maybe it's the lack of true community, maybe it's because they hate what Google has done to YouTube). Take advantage of this opportunity. Sure, YouTube may have "90% of the video traffic" or whatever their stats are nowadays, but YouTube is also saturated with crap.

You know it, I know it, there's just way too many 5 year olds who know how to use YouTube - heck, you can upload videos straight from your phone, via email, and texting! These other video sites have way less competition (even if your competition is crap), which makes it easier for you to continue to multiply your visitors from many sites instead of being lost in the big world of YouTube.

29
Submit Your Site To Directories

Good old directories. These have been around since close to the start of the internet.

As soon as people started searching for webpages online, directories were built to make it easier for people to find websites that match a specific category.

Well, they still work today. Do a search for "your website topic / main niche" + "directory". You now have thousands of directories you can submit to. Do a search for "directory" alone, and you have millions.

If you don't know what I'm talking about, here's how a directory works: You go to a directory. You navigate to the closest topic to your website. You click something like "submit url/website". Enter in your website details, and SUBMIT.

If you do this once, you won't see much of a difference to your site at all. But do this with 100 directories, and you could see some clicks and visitors coming your way. Continue to do this with other free directories, and build your back links up to 1,000+ with directories alone. You'll build up your search engine ranking, your page rank, and your visitors.

You can find many lists of free directories just by searching "free directories best list", or "free directories high pagerank". Some websites post updated lists of the best directories to submit to.

For getting traffic, there are really 2 types of directories you need to use:

1. High Page Rank, High Quality "All-around" Directories. These types of directories are like dmoz, where they have lots of visitors, high page rank, are a reputable website, and offer hundreds and thousands of different categories and sub-categories. For directories like this, make SURE they are

quality websites - because you will be focusing more on the quality of the back link, and not the direct visitors you will get from the directory.

2. Any Page Rank, Any Quality NICHE Directories. With these niche directories, you aren't worried about page rank or quality of the site (as long as it's not horrible), and are only interested in the direct traffic it can bring (and also relevancy between your site and theirs). First, search engines will see that a site similar to yours that has similar keywords is linking to you, and will rank your website accordingly for similar keywords. Also, the people who visit these one-topic, niche directories are obviously interested in this one topic greatly. So, you will probably see more traffic from these niche directories than you will in even the most popular directories with millions of links on them already.

The more directories you submit to, the more back links you'll have. The more back links you have, and the better the quality, the more visitors your website will have.

30
FREEBIE SITES

People love freebie sites for one reason, and one reason only - because there's free stuff there!

Freebies have been one of the best ways to build a community fast, and it works even better once you have a community to promote the freebie to.

That's where freebie sites come into play. Some freebie sites allow you to post a link to your website page where the freebie is located, while with other freebie sites you must give the freebie to them to place on their website (instead of your link, or both sometimes).

Choosing Your Freebie: PDF books/reports work great. So does free audio files/music, mp3, podcast. Free video, free mini-course, free anything really (make sure it is digital and able to be downloaded immediately multiple times).

Besides the type of freebie you offer, make sure you provide lots of value. Just because it's free doesn't mean everyone is going to download it! You must provide value in your freebie (remember, you are using this freebie to get people to your website by linking/mentioning it).

Posting To Freebie Sites: Search "freebies", "free stuff", "promote free stuff", "just free stuff", "free giveaways", etc. The key point in making this work is to create a viral effect. Don't post to a few freebie sites and be done. Post to 100 or more, get your freebie out there! Then, make it known to these people that they can share your freebie with whomever they want!

You can even find freebie directories, freebie facebook pages, freebie groups - just get it in front of as many eyes as possible.

31

Forum Signature Linking

Forum signature linking is when you add your website link to your forum signature to entice people to visit your website.

"But I already tried this before, it doesn't work as well as people make it look.." - Oh yeah? How many helpful posts/threads have you published in the forum? How many forums are you a part of?

The key to forum signature linking is to only promote your website in your signature, and instead of just a link, write a sentence or two about your main directive for your website - Tell these people how you can help them, or make them laugh, or make them money, whatever it is, make sure it's stated in your signature.

Now, where most go wrong: Most people join 1 or 2 forums, write about 5 or 10 comments in the forum, and wait for results. You should never be just waiting for results. Once you complete a strategy, move on to another one, and come back to the forums again later.

Start by joining 10 forums related to your niche/topic of your website. Then start writing tons of great posts in all of these forums. The key is adding tons of value to the forums, and showing people that you are an expert (or at least more of an expert) in your field. When you show that you are an expert in your field, more people will want to visit your website, and because your website link is in the signature, you'll have not only more visitors, but targeted visitors

Now as I said, you do not want to ever promote your website in an actual forum post, unless you are allowed. But even if you are allowed, a lot of the time it is looked down upon to continue to promote your website in forums. Put it this way, I have never promoted my website in any forum and have only put my website in my signature, and I've gotten more visitors than most people have using their own forum strategies.

32

POWERPOINT SLIDESHARE SITES

Powerpoint slideshare sites are amazing. So many use these types of websites to get tons of traffic to their one websites, yet I hardly see anyone promoting these sites, or even talking about them at all.

Here's how these slideshare sites work: There are hundreds of sites like this, and all of these allow you to upload your powerpoint documents for others to view online.

All you have to do is write a powerpoint document. Then, upload the document to any one of the many slideshare sites out there. The more documents you post, the more traffic you get. The more slideshare type sites you submit to, the more traffic you get. The more valuable the content, the more traffic you get.

Most of these sites allow you to post a link to your website that will show up underneath the powerpoint. It is also recommended that you provide your website URL inside your powerpoint, usually on the first and last slide will work fine.

You can decide to post brand new content, but it's even easier (and much faster) if you take videos and articles that you or others have already created, and "turn them into" powerpoint documents. It takes a lot less time to create a powerpoint slide document, and the great thing is you can continue to post the same document multiple times (on multiple sites). Powerpoints don't work like articles where if there are duplicate articles, then certain sites get penalized. With slide documents, you are able to post it to 100 sites, and never be on any search engine's "shit list".

33

FREE PRESS RELEASES

Before we get into free press releases, I just want to tell you one thing: Do not abuse press release sites. Don't post dozens of press releases every single day.

I know we've talked about quantity a lot with previous traffic strategies. With press releases, it's "sort of" the opposite. You want to use one free press release source, and allow that website to post your press release to other websites.

Let's talk about what exactly a press release really means. With press releases, you want the PRESS and the WORLD to know about something big you've just done/completed/published/changed/etc. Press releases are more about news, not a tutorial or article or anything like that. A lot of companies usually publish press releases when they launch a new product, or feature on their website, also big events and happenings with websites and businesses find their way into press releases.

So, what type of content is "press release worthy"?

I would say any time you make major updates to your site, write a huge amazing article that other people will love, any time you create a product, course, even freebies work great for press releases.

Another quick tip, make sure your press releases are short and sweet. People read dozens of these every day (actually, they GET dozens per day, and probably only read a few). You want to make sure it is short and sweet, to the point, gives all the details of your big news for you website, and provides a clear call-to-action, which will get people interested in your website. Then, when they see your website link at the bottom of the press release, they'll gladly click on it to find out more.

34
Traffic Exchanges

Traffic exchanges are one of my favorite ways to get traffic.

I don't care what else I say/said in this book, traffic exchanges are the EASIEST way to get traffic. The only problem is, this traffic isn't going to be as targeted as you'd like - in fact it's not really targeted at all.

Usually you are going to have to bring in 10s of thousands of visitors into your website before you get anyone becoming a return visitor, subscriber, or buyer.

Traffic exchanges work like this: You go from website to website, looking at each website for 5 - 10 seconds each (some more, some less), and each website you view, depending on the credit distribution, you will get visitors to your website.

Now, the reason this type of traffic strategy gives you untargeted visitors is because the people that are looking at your website/page are only viewing your page so that they get more views and visitors on their own website.

If all you want is visitors, no matter how untargeted they are, traffic exchanges are the way to go. You can honestly get 10,000 - 20,000 visitors PER DAY by surfing around on traffic exchanges for 3 to 4 hours per day (yeah, this is easy traffic).

A strategy I like to use with traffic exchanges is to join 10 exchanges, open each traffic exchange in it's own tab (use a tabbed browser), then go tab to tab clicking "next" on each exchange, and you will have 10 times more visitors than if you only used one traffic exchange.

If you DO care about targeted traffic, and care about getting future traffic, email subscribers, buyers, etc., you will need to do a little more work with the types of pages that you show. It's easiest to get targeted traffic and return traffic by offering some sort of freebie on these traffic exchanges, and instead of linking directly to your homepage, or your site with sidebars and banner, it's better to show them what's called a "splash page", where you show these visitors one thing that you'd like them to do/have. You could give them a free report, you could provide your email subscription form to allow people to become an email subscriber to your list.

Just make sure you are providing value, and that you have a good enough offer so that you have a higher percentage of these traffic exchange visitors returning to your website at a later date.

35
SEO - Search Engine Optimization

Again, this is one of those traffic strategies that I could write an entire book about.

Search Engine Optimization. You've heard about it. You've probably also heard about all the failures you could experience with SEO.

Many people love SEO because it allows them to optimize everything ON your website without using any other traffic strategies so that your website show up in search engine results.

More and more people are stopping their SEO strategies (or not focusing as much on them) becaues of the search engine updating their algorithms all the time. More people are focused on other traffic strategies, because when search engines update their algorithms, and your website's pages start to drop in search engine results, you'll have to go back into your website, and re-optimize EVERYTHING - pages, categories, tags, titles, images, content. You really always have to be ahead of the game, and on top of new SEO practices.

So, because SEO is changing all the time, I'm just going to list a few of the main things you must do to optimize your website.

First, make sure your site stays on topic. If you are going to make a website, make sure that all of the articles, pages, videos, keywords, titles, and content of the site all relate to one main topic or niche. When you jump around from topic to topic, search engines will not know what your site is about. However, if you stick to a topic, say for instance "painting or art", you can then form your website's content to match that specific topic or niche.

I know we talked about this before, but start using long tail keywords! These will optimize your site beyond belief, as they will get you visitors that are searching for a specific topic, and there is a lot less competition for these long tail keywords (of course on the other side of that, there is also a lot less searches for these keywords).

Above and beyond all, make sure you are at least optimizing for keywords (use the Google Keyword Tool to find good keyword ideas), sprinkle the keywords around your content, titles, tags, and pages.

36

Update Your Site Frequently

In no way is this some sort of secret strategy. It is more common sense than anything.

But, the fact of the matter is, by updating your site frequently, you will have way more visitors coming into your site, and search engines will love you. And as you found out in the previous chapter, it is sometimes hard to get search engines to love you, or even like you for that matter!

So, whether it is a video, article, a tutorial, a book or a freebie, always make sure you update your site frequently - all the time - as much as you can!

When you update your site or blog frequently, search engines will take notice and will reward you with higher search engine rankings. This is because, in the mind of the search engines, any blog that is updated frequently looks like they have new things to share with the world, and search engines would rather show that above other results.

Here are some strategies on how you can update your site frequently and much easier than any other post on your blog:

First, go take a look at some of the other blogs in your niche and find out what they are talking about. You can then form your new posts and articles and make them relate to the types of things that other people in your niche are talking about.

Another easy strategy that sort of goes with the first one is to review blog posts from other blogs. Just write a short blog post talking a little bit about someone else's article and then provide a link to their article.

One more way to update your site frequently is to embed other people's videos into your blog posts. Most people who post videos to YouTube allow you to post their video on your blog. You should be taking advantage of this. You can either write a short description of the video or post the video and transcribe it so that there is new content in your post.

37

Use Viral Content

I know this is an old-school term, but let's talk about viral content.

What is viral content?

Viral content is basically any type of content that people find interesting enough to share with large amounts of people. It could be a viral video, a viral PDF download, but really anything that is easy to see, get, or download.

Let's talk about different types of viral content, as well as a few different strategies for getting traffic to your website from this viral content.

First let's talk about viral PDFs, otherwise known as viral e-books. It's a lot easier to write an e-book than you think. Think of some great life-changing content, write between 5 to 10 or maybe even 20 pages of content in a word document, then save it as a PDF. There you go, you just wrote your first viral e-book. Of course, I assume you know that you must include your website link a few times in the viral e-book in order to get traffic to your website.

My final tip for viral e-books is: Make sure you make it clear at the beginning and end of the book that anyone and everyone is free to send the book to anyoneone they want.

Besides viral PDFs, you could also go the viral video route. In order to make a video go viral, it must: be shocking, include someone getting hurt, be the most inspiring thing you've ever seen, be controversial, be a slap in your face, OR be extremely funny.

Come on, you've seen videos that go viral, and then they promote some website, and sometimes the video has nothing to do with the website. But the fact that 10 million people watched a video, and 5% clicked on the website link, that gives you half a million website visitors. Cool, right? And of course, you could use some of the traffic strategies in this book to give your viral video a jump start of views.

We'll talk about viral articles in a future chapter.

38

OFFLINE PROMOTION TACTICS

Besides all of these online traffic strategies, I am now going to tell you about some off-the-wall off-line promotion tactics for getting visitors to your website.

As you will find out, it is harder to get website traffic using these off-line promotion tactics, but when used correctly, they can work wonders. I'll go ahead and list off a handful of off-line promotion tactics that I have used to get website traffic.

1. Bumper Stickers - Don't tell me you've never read a bumper sticker out loud. Make a funny, interesting, or crazy looking bumper sticker (or any type of car decal), and put it on your car. Heck, you could even sell these or give them away to friends.

2. Business Cards - I don't even care if you don't have money to buy professional business cards - you don't need em'. I've seen people who cut their own business cards using white construction paper, then writing their website URL on both sides, that's it, as simple as that. Then, give your "website cards" to your friends, family, anyone you think would be interested in your site - anyone you meet! (I've seen website cards on my windshield after leaving the bank)

3. More crazier ideas - Since I don't have too much experience with the following, I figured I'd at least list them all so you can have something to go from (if you want to go the off-line promotion route).

Play music or entertain people on the street corner, and wear a shirt with your website name on it. Instead of asking for money, put a sign with an arrow down saying "take my card", with 1,000 or so website cards (yeah, I just thought of that one). Design and/or make your own t-shirts. Give em away, sell em, whatever - just get people wearing them. Word of mouth also works great. Tell people about your

99 Ways To Flood Your Website With Traffic

website if they seem interested in it. Get a TV Ad Spot, get a radio ad spot (you can find cheap spots, just ask around and do some research).

With offline promotion, you have to think big. Don't just place one bumper sticker on one car, give hundreds away to people who you know will wear it with pride. Don't just give out a few business cards here and there. Instead of giving out one business card, give out 5 to one person, tell them to share it around. Put your cards in those business raffle jars.

Here's one more sneaky strategy I used with one of my first websites: There were tons of businesses that had those clear acrylic table toppers/covers that you could put pictures under. Well, I also started to see some business cards under these as well. So, I made up my own batch of 50 business cards, sneakily placed a couple under each acrylic table topper, and only had 6 cards left by the end of the day. Over the next week, my website traffic tripled. I'm definitely not saying this will work in the new age, that was about 8 years ago - just thought I'd share a fun story.

39

URL In Email Signatures

This strategy is really easy to implement, and can be completed in the next two minutes.

Whether you have a complete email list, or if you just use email personally, you need to start using email signatures. Most people just put their name in their email signatures. But even worse than just having a name as an email signature is putting tons of links to all the different stuff of yours online.

Again, you have to keep things simple. I keep things as simple as providing my first and last name followed by a link to my website in my signature. The only other extra thing you could add to your email signature is what your website is about. But again, keep this short and simple.

Of course having your website URL in your email signature will never get you any website traffic unless you start sending some emails. So, send some emails to friends, maybe send some emails to some family members, you could even send emails to people you don't know. That is all I'm going to talk about regarding email website traffic for now, and I'll be talking about other email website traffic strategies in future chapters.

40
FREE CONTEST OR GIVEAWAY

Free contests and giveaways do take some work, but they are one of the most fun traffic strategies online.

Here's how free contests and giveaways work. First of all, you need to know the difference between contests and giveaways. A contest is when you have set instructions and rules, and people must do something in order to join, and then the best one is picked by you or a panel of judges (of your choosing). A giveaway is when anyone can enter, and a winner is chosen randomly out of a hat.

I would say contests are more fun than giveaways, but giveaways are much more easier, so we'll be talking about giveaways for the most part.

First, you need a prize. Sure, you could go out and buy something or maybe purchase a gift card and give a physical product away. But, there are also ways you can give away something for free that you don't have to pay for. Some examples of things you could give away for free that you don't have to pay for include a video shout out, a free one month ad on your website, or even a product or book that you are selling online currently.

Next, you need to create a giveaway page on your website, tell people how to join (could be by entering their email to join a giveaway list, or commenting on your giveaway page, then sharing the page - or something like that. Get creative.

Once you have all the rules, dates, and page set up, it's time to promote your giveaway. Again, do some searches for giveaway sites online, as well as sites that list freebies, giveaways, and contests. Tell people about it on facebook, post it on facebook pages for giveaways, tweet it! Give people an extra entry for sharing the giveaway, or making a video about it, or posting a link, etc. Think outside the box, promote your giveaway like crazy, and you might just fry your web server from all the traffic you get (good times).

41

POLL AND SURVEY GIVEAWAYS

I wanted to put poll and survey giveaways directly after free contests and giveaways because they differ a lot.

Instead of having just one prize and just one winner, you will be giving away something to anyone and everyone who participates in your poll or survey.

Again, it's easiest to give away something like a PDF document - you could call it a "short report" or a "secret strategy", or something that gets people excited about what you are giving them.

For this book, I'll give you a prime example of a poll giveaway:

- You like making music, beats, instrumentals, and your site is called TheMusicMakingWebsite.com.

- You create 2 beats, 5 drum loops, and an HD video on how to sell beats easily online (5 - 10 minute video).

- You put all of this into a folder, ZIP it up, and add it to your file manager (either directly on your host's server, or using FTP).

- You create a download link for this ZIP folder, then create a "poll/giveaway" page.

- Now this is the only step you have to do a quick search. Search for the most reputable free "poll" website/service. Make sure the poll service allows you to post the poll on your website, and once someone chooses A, B, C, or D (or more choices), they are shown your download link.

- Put the poll on your website. Get traffic to your poll. Again, have some sharing buttons on this page, and entice people to share this around. It could say "show your friends the awesome package you just got!" with some facebook and twitter share links.

- Then, promote it like crazy.

You can decide yourself if you want to have a poll or survey that has an end to date, or you can let your poll continue for the entire life of your site. Either way, it doesn't matter too much. If you decide to take the poll away, and then show the results, and offer your download absolutely free on that page, go ahead. If you want to end it, and SELL your giveaway at a later date, you can do that too. Or, you can leave the poll up, and allow the results to continue to change, and keep watching people download your free gift.

ONE MORE IMPORTANT NOTE: If you want even more traffic, make sure you include your website name in the giveaway content - either make a new document with your website link, or say your website in the video, or name your zip folder your website name. Anything that gets the name of your website in front of your viewers eyes will help you get more frequent visitors to your website.

42

Pinterest and Similar Sites

The reason I titled this chapter "Pinterest and Similar Sites" is because Pinterest is a new website and I'm not sure how long it's going to be around. However, even if Pinterest isn't around, there are still going to be dozens and probably hundreds of sites just like it.

So, what is Pinterest, and how can it help you?

On Pinterest you are allowed to "pin" (post) websites, photos, products, and other fun things you find online straight to Pinterest. Then, other people are able to vote your pin UP or DOWN. The more it gets pinned/voted up, the more people see your pin. The more interesting the offer/website/image is, the more people will click on it, giving you more website traffic.

I think you understand how Pinterest works, so I'm just going to leave you with some insight in this chapter:

New sites that come up in the world and gain popularity fast are great for you and me, but it seems like every time a new big site is launched and starts gaining popularity, more people find ways to "abuse" the system. I'm talking about those "secret hacks to millions of views". You shouldn't worry about secret hacks, as they disappear quicker than they appear. You should worry more about new trending sites that come into play, and take advantage of these sites while others are still fiddling with facebook and twitter.

The more you stay on top of new websites, new practices, and new traffic generation tactics, and the more you think outside the box in terms of getting website and blog visitors, the better chance you have at being one of the first founders of the site. Put it this way: A year ago, I joined a new site that allows me to sell my beats online. When I joined, there were exactly 3 people selling their beats on this site. So, I posted

99 Ways To Flood Your Website With Traffic

50 of my beats, and basically owned most of the site's real estate. Then, as hundreds and thousands of new producers entered this selling space, I was the one at the top, who knew how the site worked, who knew the ins and outs of selling my beats.

And it was all because I was on top of things and got in early.

43

Dynamic Content On Site For Autopilot Traffic

Let's talk about dynamic content VS static content.

Static content is what most people use on their sites and is basically just the webpages, articles, and other site pages that once they are published, they never change.

Now, static content is good for a few reasons, the main reason being that search engines and other people that visit your site will see the same content on the same page they visited weeks ago, and it will be easier to rank in search engines for this content.

Dynamic content brings new fuel to the table. Think of the dynamic content like Facebook. Someone on the other side of your country can view the same exact page as you on Facebook, yet they could be seeing completely different content.

Types of dynamic content include: comments (that update everytime someone comments/writes on your page), user profiles (like forums), member pages, top commenters, and also plug-ins in general.

You can go ahead and do a search for different types of dynamic content, however, there are a few things you should look out for. If you are new to dynamic content, it can very well put a much larger load to your website server. When I have ads, dynamic pages that change all the time, polls, comments, and many different plug-ins, I find that instead of having 1 visitor, 1 pageview, and 1 hit, I instead have 1 visitor, 5 pageviews, and 30 or 40 hits.

My tip to you for dynamic content: Install one plug-in at a time. Don't create too many dynamic pages at once, as you could fry your server and get your website temporarily shut down. Take things one step at a time, and if your website starts loading too slow, or you have to start paying more money each month for hosting, you can tone down the dynamic content.

All in all, dynamic content brings you more visitors, more pageviews, and most importantly, MUCH more interaction. And that's what you want on your site, a community.

44

Using Google+

Google+ is Google's "social network", which allows you to add people to circles, and allows other people to add you to their own circles.

Every time I post something online, I +1 it, and see hundreds of visitors pouring into my site. However, you might be thinking, "everytime I post to Google+, I NEVER get traffic, why?"

First, you need to start adding hundreds of relevant people to your circles. Again, search around the site, and see what people are talking about. If you have a website about gardening, and you see a complete group of 30 people talking about gardening, ADD THEM ALL TO YOUR "GARDENING" CIRCLE.

Then, communicate with these people - don't just spam them with links. Comment on other people's posts and Plus Ones. When you show people you care, more people will be willing and wanting to see what you have to post.

And once again, above all else, provide lots of value. If you just link to your post or video on your site saying "go check this out!!", you may only get a few visitors. But if you post something that actually HELPS people, or makes people laugh, or evoke emotion in people, the sky is the limit - you could have 500 visitors instantly from a helpful +1.

Too many people try to find work-arounds to networks like this, and then show you how you can scheme the system. Instead of worrying about how many links you are posting, and how many visitors you get from each post, try to NOT focus on website visitors. I know that sounds weird, but trust me, the more you look like a real person and not a robot posting links, the more interaction you will get on your posts and shares.

45
Get Traffic From LinkedIn

I'm going to keep this chapter brief, as it goes along the same way as other social networks.

LinkedIn is a website that I believe is going to be around for a long while, so it's important to mention it in it's entirety in this book.

Besides the sharing, having a community, helping people, looking like a human, and interacting with others, you must look at LinkedIn from a slightly different perspective.

LinkedIn is all about business contacts. It's all about "who is this person, what have they done, what can they do for me?".

So, when you are becoming friends with other business contacts on LinkedIn, find out what "business" these people are in. If you make sock puppet tutorials, find people who are in the "arts/crafts" world, and add them to your network. If you make music, find other people who make music.

I find that this works even better if you find people in the same CORE niche, but not in the same MICRO niche. This means if you are a music producer from San Francisco, don't JUST add other music producers from San Francisco. Find music artists (who need beats), music promoters (who can promote your beats), film makers (who can use your instrumental music for movies). I think you get the idea. Find people who are not only relevant to your niche, but people who are a complement to your niche and business.

46

Article Submission

Article submission used to be huge years ago. Now, when I say used to be huge years ago, it's still huge, but just not in the eyes of the "guru marketers" out there.

Nowadays you'll find more and more people who tell you that article marketing doesn't work at all. The only thing I have to say to that is, they are just not doing it the correct way.

With article marketing, you submit articles to different article directories and post your website link in the resource box to allow people to visit your website after reading your content.

Some people will tell you that there are too many articles out there, others will tell you that there are too many people posting articles to have any sort of effect with article marketing. The reason most of these people fail with article marketing is because they focus more on the visitors and statistics from article marketing, and fail to provide value to the person reading the article.

Guess what? The people reading your articles are humans!!! Make sure you act like one. Don't just take someone else's article, rearrange some of the content, and then repost the same article to dozens of article directories. Instead, focus on the actual people that are searching and finding your article.

Article Submissions Help In 2 Ways:

1. It gives you direct visitors. These are the people that search for a solution to their problem, find your article, and it helped them so much that they decide to visit your website (your website link should ONLY be in the resource box at the bottom of each article).

2. It gives you more link juice. The more articles you post, the more your website link shows up on other websites. Post 1 article to 1 directory, and

99 Ways To Flood Your Website With Traffic

have 1 back link from 1 site. Post 10 articles on 10 directories, and have 10 back links (or more) from 10 or more sites. The more back links you have from article directories, the higher search engines will rank you.

Get out there, find a good handful of article directories, and start posting!

47

CRAIGSLIST TRAFFIC

Now, this craigslist traffic strategy is pretty sneaky, so if you feel like you don't want to use this, move onto the next traffic strategy.

However, every single time I use this craigslist traffic strategy, I receive thousands of visitors to my website every single time.

I bet you've probably bought something on craigslist before. You've probably even sold something on craigslist before. What you probably don't know, is that you can get tons of website traffic from craigslist.

Also, because craigslist is updated so frequently, Google and other search engines tend to spider their website all the time. This means that if you make a post on craigslist with your website link in it, Google will take notice, find your website, and rank you better in their search engine.

Here is my Craigslist Traffic Strategy:

- First, if you have something for free on your website, post it in the "free" section on Craigslist. People look for freebies all day. Post your freebie to a few different cities (make sure your posts aren't duplicates, or all of your posts will go to "spam" and be flagged/removed), and multiply your traffic as many times as you want.

- Next, have you ever looked at the "jobs/gigs" area? If you have a blog, you can post something in the "writer gigs" section, and ask people to write for your blog. Post a link to your blog to "allow people to preview where their articles will be posted", and provide an email address for them to send you their intent to be a blogger/writer for you.

You don't even have to look at these emails if you don't want (although if you want more content, I would say go ahead and accept the free articles that people give you). Oh yeah, you need to make sure you include the "no-pay" feature. Don't tell people you'll pay them $10 for each article when you know you have no money.

Are you starting to see how this works? Again, it's all about thinking outside the box. Go to every section on Craigslist, and start going through a thought process of "how can I post my website link here, AND not get flagged/removed/banned from craigslist?".

I said this would be sneaky. If you find that your posts are getting removed too often, STOP immediately. Make sure you take breaks from craigslist posting, because if Craigslist (and it's users) find you to be a menace to the site, and a "spammer"/"scammer", you could get your IP banned from using the site. And that's never good... When your IP is banned, that means you can no longer use Craigslist from the computer you were using (and if you still live at home, it could ban your entire household from using the site).

So, take caution, take things one step at a time, and the more you post, the higher search engine rankings and more visitors you will get.

48

USE THE GOOGLE KEYWORD TOOL

I mentioned the Google Keyword Tool in a few previous chapters, and I think it deserves its own chapter because of all of the great things that can come from it.

First, do a search for the Google keyword tool, enter in the captcha, and get started. With the Google Keyword Tool, you are able to enter in as many keywords as you want, and then Google pumps out 100s of relevant keyword ideas for you to use (that people are actually searching for!). Google actually tells you about how many people search for certain keywords each month, as well as the competition for each keyword.

Use this tool to your advantage. Spend a couple hours using the Google keyword tool, and you will come up with hundreds and sometimes thousands of different keyword ideas to use on your website.

Here's a quick crash-course to using this tool properly:

- Start by entering in your main, core keyword. This should be something like "technology", or "gardening", or "music".

- Now you'll find hundreds of keywords that relate to your main keyword, but are longer-tail, with less competition.

- Don't stop here. Start copying these longer-tail keywords, and run these through the keyword tool.

- Now you have even LONGER tail keywords. You'll start to see that although the searches for these keywords go down, the competition goes down as well.

99 Ways To Flood Your Website With Traffic

- The key is finding keywords that have almost 0 competition, but still generate 100s or 1000s of searches each month.

Once you have a list of 100 or 200 keywords, it's time to put them to good use!

If you have a keyword that gets 5,000 searches a month with no competition, you should write an article with that keyword as your title. Because there is no competition, you can be almost 100% positive that you will get this article to the front page of Google with little promotional work.

Now, if you find other keywords that DO have higher competition, you can very well still use these. But, instead of titling your articles with these keywords, start to sprinkle around these keywords in your future articles (and past articles if you feel like it). Take for instance the keyword "lose 10 pounds". There are millions of people using this keyword, making it harder to rank your site/page for the keyword by just including it once. But when search engines see the keyword "lose 10 pounds" 50 times on your site, sprinkled around between tags, titles, articles, and pages, you'll start to rank higher for that keyword, as well as keywords similar to it.

This does take some time to research, but keyword research is something you should definitely be doing from time to time.

49
Google Bookmarks

Yep, another Google tool, fresh of the press. Before getting into the details, let me tell you: Make Google your FRIEND. Google will be around FOREVER. Do you really want to piss off the biggest website in the world? Of course not. Learn to use the tools that Google gives you, because when you do, Google rewards you.

So, Google Bookmarks - ever heard of it? You've probably heard of bookmarking, and I already told you about pinging. Google Bookmarks brings both of these into one (this is just my own perspective).

When you bookmark your site, or even just one of your pages using Google Bookmarks, you are doing 2 things:

1. You are showing Google that this site/page is important to you.

2. You are showing PEOPLE that this site/page is important to you.

Go ahead and bookmark all your important pages on your website, including the home page. Then, tell your friends, family, and social buddies to bookmark your site as well.

The more times people "Google Bookmark" your page, the more Google will check out your site (in the background using their algorithmic spider bots), and the higher your site will rank.

So, bookmark your homepage now. Then tell 5 friends to bookmark it using the same strategy you used. Make it known directly on your site for people to bookmark your pages. The more it's bookmarked with Google, the more Google likes you. And the more Google likes you and your website, the more traffic and promotion you get from the wonderful search engine.

50
GET DOFOLLOW BACK LINKS

Okay, you are officially HALF WAY THROUGH THIS BOOK!

As you are probably noticing, ALL of these traffic tactics intertwine with each other. Each one can help another one out. It's when you start using all of these tactics, that your traffic will just continue to multiply, because most of these (once they are set up), continue to work on auto-pilot.

Just like this chapter, "Get DoFollow Back Links". We've talked about back links in general, we've also talked about blog commenting - this goes with both of those strategies, as well as dozens of others.

The difference between DoFollow and NoFollow:

Both DoFollow and NoFollow back links are shown the same way on websites. It's just a link that someone can click on and get to another webpage. These two work the same way for humans, but for search engines, are complete polar opposites.

- NoFollow back links means that search engines will not spider the link, or even look at it, let alone know that it's there. With nofollow links, you are completely dependant on people clicking on the link to view your website.

- DoFollow back links look the same, act the same for humans, but differ greatly for search engines. With DoFollow backlinks, search engines and other algorithmic sites online will view this back link, spider it, and rank the linked site accordingly.

Search for "DoFollow blogs" or "DoFollow comments" in your favorite serach engine. You'll find lists of sites, blogs, and services that give you dofollow back links.

You can focus on both nofollow AND dofollow backlinks, but you will be doing a bigger service to your site and business by focusing MORE on DoFollow.

51

STUMBLEUPON TRAFFIC

Who knows how long this site will be live for. All I know is, right now it's one of my "big" traffic sources I use.

StumbleUpon is a social bookmarking website that allows you to "like" pages. The more a page is liked, the more it shows up when people "Stumble" to a new site on StumbleUpon.

Instead of posting new content to another website, StumbleUpon shows your actual website's/page's content. So if you have a great blog post on your blog, you can "stumble like" it. Then, if others like it, they'll continue to vote it up. The more it gets voted up, the more it gets shown to other people.

Although you can't expect every single one of your articles to go viral on StumbleUpon, I suggest you post every single one of your articles and pages to stumbleupon, because you never know what sort of content others will find useful. Or can you?

Here are the types of content that tend to go viral on StumbleUpon:

- Real stories that touch people's hearts.

- Shocking content.

- Extremely funny content.

- Content that helps people more than any other content could have.

The best part about StumbleUpon is you never have to say "go visit my website!" - They are already on your website. So just create some life-changing content on your site, and STUMBLE.

52
START CONTROVERSY

I put this traffic tactic right after StumbleUpon, because controversial topics work GREAT for this bookmarking site.

Who cares if 50% love you, and 50% hate you. Would you rather have 10 people love your "okay" content and 0 people hate it, or 50,000 people love your controversy, and 50,000 hate it? The choice is yours.

When you start controversy, you lift people's emotions to all time highs. People feel like they need to comment. People feel like they need to show this "stupid article" to all their friends.

But guess what? Even if all these people hate you, you're going to be old news TOMORROW. However, the traffic still came through, and now your site will rank higher than it ever has before.

Write about politics. Write about what you hate. Write rants. GO CRAZY! GO AGAINST SOMETHING! BE A DAMN MENACE!!

Write about things that get people heated. Get people heated, and they'll exchange their heat to your website - making your website HOT baby!

53

MAKE YOUR WEBSITE
USER-FRIENDLY

50% of the readers of this book will skip this chapter (just a guess).

The reason I say this is because it sounds too simple, and isn't a "traffic hack" or anything like that. However, it is more important than most traffic tactics.

Most people focus on TRAFFIC TRAFFIC TRAFFIC, and then find out that the traffic comes and goes extremely quick.

To ensure your website generates future, residual visitors, you need to have a user-friendly website. Sure, you may pump a thousand visitors into your site within a few hours, but after that, they are gone... unless you have a site that makes people want to return!

Make your navigation area easy to get around. Remember when I talked about dynamic content? Use it! Tell people about upcoming content on your website, get people interested!

Add images, make your content easy to read. Make it easy for people to save your site so they come back in the future.

The more user-friendly you make your website, the more your business and website will succeed. And when you make it easy on your human visitors, all of those "search engine bots" will take notice, and rank your site even higher.

Bottom line: Focus more on your human visitors, and the rankings and search engine traffic will follow. Do it the other way around, and you'll have more complications and struggles than you can handle.

54

SEND EMAILS TO PEOPLE WHO KNOW YOU

Mom, dad, brother, sister, cousins, extended family, facebook friends, social buddies, online buddies, business contacts - these are all people you know.

Put together a list of everyone's email that KNOW YOU, and send them your website!

You never want to spam the people who know you. Don't send them every single article. But every once and awhile, send a useful article or a link to your website. You can even ask them, "How does my site look? I'm working hard on it every day!"

Since these people are the closest people to you, they are more likely to visit your website, share it around, and are more willing to help you with promoting your website!

In my early website days, I underestimated the power of friends and family. I thought, "they have no interest in this stuff". Boy was I wrong. I found out that my uncle had a friend in the music biz, so when my uncle saw my website, he forwarded the email to his buddy, then he sent it to his list, and I had hundreds of new visitors within days.

Even if you don't want to update your friends and family, at least send them your website link once to let them know what you are doing. More visitors, more sharing, it all helps.

55

SEND EMAILS TO PEOPLE WHO DON'T KNOW YOU

Besides sending emails to people who know you, you can also send emails to people who DON'T KNOW YOU.

Do not spam. Like above, you don't want to continue to send people emails if they haven't "opted-in" to an email list of yours.

Like before, make a list of emails of people who own websites/services/businesses similar to your own.

But, instead of sending this entire list the same email, personalize each one. If someone has a popular website that gets 100X more visitors than you, tell them you enjoy their site, and have been a long time visitor. Mention a few things that this person has personally helped you with. THANK them.

Then, tell them about your website. Besides your website, tell them who you are, what you do, and how you strive to [enter your own motto here].

Most of these people will ignore your emails. Some will read them. Even fewer will take a look at your site. And even fewer than that will share your site with others.

That's right, this isn't a "cut n' dry" formula. But when this does work, it works like a charm. You'll find some of these "big guys and girls" will tweet your website link, or share one of your articles with their list, they may even comment and become a future visitor themselves!

56

ADD A "BOOKMARK THIS SITE" BUTTON TO YOUR SITE/BLOG

Now, we've already talked about bookmarking your site through different bookmarking sources. It's now time to add a "bookmark this site" button to your blog.

Go ahead and do a search for bookmark buttons. If you use a popular blogging platforms like WordPress, there are thousands of plug-ins that have bookmarking buttons that you can place on your website.

Add to your bookmark button to the most prime position on your website. Usually, this will be at the very top of your website.

Before, people would visit your site, and if they want to visit it in the future, they will have to personally search for your website or remember your website name and type it into the URL box. With a bookmark button on your site, people are now able to save your website in their bookmarks so that they can view your website in the future.

This not only helps with getting return visitors who bookmark your website, but search engines will also rank you higher, bringing you more visitors in the future.

57

GET AN EMAIL LIST

I have already talked to you about email in previous chapters. Now it's time to talk about getting yourself a professional email list.

Ask any online marketer, and they will tell you that email lists are their #1 traffic source.

Now, in order to get an email list started, you will need some start-up money. The only reason I included this in the "free traffic" part of this book is because it's not buying a specific amount of visitors or advertising.

For most email autoresponder services (like AWeber, MailChimp, etc.), there is a one time fee to set up your email list. Then, you only have to make future payments once your list gets HUGE (into the 10s of thousands of subscribers).

This is good because if you have a small list, you might not be paying much at all. Then, once your list gets bigger, you'll have small payments to make, but with a list this big, you should be making your money back through monetizing your list with affiliate offers, your own products, advertising on your website, etc.

First do a search for email autoresponders. Join a company (I use AWeber right now). Set up an email list. Make an opt-in form.

An example of an opt-in form is like the one at the beginning and end of this book. The publisher of this book, Web Core Media and 99for99books.com, have an email list set up for you to join. Go ahead and join if you want, you can get our books for free in the future ;) You can also see how an email autoresponder works.

With an autoresponder, you are able to have set emails that get sent to your list on timed intervals. You can also "broadcast" single emails to your list as well.

99 Ways To Flood Your Website With Traffic

Put it this way: If your YouTube account gets disabled, all your subscribers are gone. If your twitter account gets suspended, all your followers are gone. If any other website you are a part of goes haywire, all your content on that site is lost.

But by having an email list, you have 100% rights to the emails on your list, and they'll never just "shut down". Almost all autoresonder companies keep caches of your list, so even if something goes wrong, they still have backups for you to use.

When people join your list, you can now send them articles of yours, videos, products that you make money from, videos, and any other types of content.

So, if you have some money (right now you can try AWeber for a month for $1, then after the month, a yearly or monthly fee depending on your list sizes), get an email list now.

58

PUT YOUR OPT-IN FORM EVERYWHERE ON YOUR SITE

So you've got an autoresponder, your emails set up, and some great content to send to your list, but your list is nearly empty.

This is where your opt-in form comes in to play. Your placement and quantity of your opt-in forms on your site is a big help to traffic generation.

Here's a hypothetical example (sort of like a "here's what could happen if this happens"):

1,000 visitors to your site X 1% opt-in/subcribe = 10 subscribers

So if you get 1,000 visitors to your site each day, you could have 300 subscribers in a month.

But what if you put your opt-in form everywhere on your site. As you'll guess, more people will subscribe to your email list.

Here's some good places to put your opt-in form:

- At the top of one of your sidebars
- As a pop-up when they first get to your site
- As a pop-up when they are about to exit your site
- Right above or below the comment section
- At the bottom of every page.

99 Ways To Flood Your Website With Traffic

By having your opt-in box in many different places (and even changing the design up a bit for each placement), you can expect your email subscriber/member count to rise.

Here's some more numbers:

1,000 visitors X 10% opt-in rate = 100 subscribers

10,000 visitors X 15% opt-in rate = 1,500 subscribers

Here's a "crazy" one (but not impossible by any means):

1 million visitors X 20% opt-in rate = 200,000 subscribers

It's all about adding value, giving away freebies, putting your site out there, and when you get your email list into the 100s of thousands (6 digits +), the possibilities are endless. Imagine being able to send an email saying anything you want to 100,000+ people instantly.

Well, that all starts with putting your opt-in box everywhere, to get a higher percentage of visitors becoming email subscribers.

59
Create A Content Plan

This is where I would have started the book, but I didn't want to sound like every other book that say "it all starts with content" / "content is king".

But the truth is, if you want to continue to get traffic to your website all the time, you need to have a great content plan.

I hope you took the tip of using the Google Keyword Tool. But that's just the start. You can research keywords all day long, but if you can't present that information to your audience in the best, user-friendly way possible, these visitors are never going to visit your site again.

When I had the idea of starting a few different blogs on topics I knew eh... a little bit about, I put together a 10 page content plan.

Here's some things you should start thinking about:

- Put together a list of articles you want to write about.

- Have long lists of keywords. Put them in order of long-tail to short-tail, or based on competition/searches, etc.

- Write down your prime motives for your website or blog. Do you want to teach people skills? Make them laugh? Having motives for your site keeps people coming back, because you are no longer "some random site", you are the "coolest site that has one specific goal in place".

- Will you start a podcast? Maybe just articles at the start? How 'bout a video series? Start writing down what media you are going to have on your website.

99 Ways To Flood Your Website With Traffic

Before you worry about traffic, make sure you have a completely amazing site ready for this traffic to view. Start comparing your website to the most popular websites. What features/design/content do they have that you don't?

60
STARTING CHAIN REACTIONS

Here I want to talk about something not so specific. This traffic strategy works with many other traffic strategies put together.

Starting chain reactions happens when a lot of things are put into place first. You must have sharing/bookmark buttons on your site. You must have an e-mail list. You should build up your twitter followers, facebook fans/likes, everything you can.

You also need to have valuable content. Think about what I said earlier: Start controversy, change people's lives, post something hilarious.

When you put all of these together, you can start a huge snowball of traffic that could go on for days at a time. The key thing to note here is: The bigger your following/list/subscribers, the easier it is to get the snowball rolling.

Here's some examples:

- You post an amazing article with a freebie attached to the end. You share it with 1,000 twitter followers, 500 facebook friends, 3,000 facebook fans, 500 email subscribers, and 1,000 to other networks. That's over 6,000 immediate people able to see this amazing article and freebie (make sure you have a JUICY title). Let's say 10% check out your article - that's 600 visitors. If you have sharing buttons in place, they can share it with tons of their friends. Let's say of the 600, 10% share it. That's 60 people sharing your article and freebie. If those 60 people have a similar viewership to you (let's say each sends/shares this to 500 people), that's 30,000 people getting your article shared to (and if 10% of them view it, that's 3,000 more visitors!). It can keep going for awhile at this rate.

- You post 10 free beats on a page. You share it with a combined 100,000 people. 10% visit your site = 10,000 visitors. If 10% of those share it, that's 1,000 shares (sent to average 500 people) = 500,000 shares (X 10% click to

99 Ways To Flood Your Website With Traffic

see your page = 50,000 more viewers). And again, it will continue from here.

As you can see, the bigger the snowball starts, the easier it is to get going. So build up your following, make great content, share it around, and start a chain reaction of website visitors.

61

CREATE A PRODUCT (PAID OR FREE)

This strategy is one that many don't use simply because they are too scared.

Whether you set-up a paypal or clickbank order form for a paid product, or if you are just giving away your product for free, BOTH WORK GREAT.

Now, of course giving away your product without getting their email address is okay, but not recommended. I recommend setting up an email list specifically for this one product.

Once you create a product, you can then promote the product (if it's free, it's even better). This gets people buzzing about your website and product, and gets people talking. Even better, get some testimonials on your product, and even more people will get excited and check it out.

Like I said above, you should never let your visitors have a product until you have their email address. You can do this by setting up an email autoresponder like I told you in a previous chapter, and making the "welcome email" include the download link to your product.

When you are giving people a product (again, this works better if it's free), they are happy to give you their email address, especially if they know the product should be worth more than you are giving it to them for.

When you build up your email list (you can get 10,000 - 100,000 emails from one product), you can then promote more paid products to this list, or even just email them for future articles and content on your website.

62

Free Classified Ads

I know I previously talked about Craigslist, but it's important to start making your way around the other free classified ad sites out there.

Just search "free classified ads", and you'll have thousands to choose from. Usually, the ones on the first page of results get the most visitors, so start there.

I see classfieds every day. It's important to make your ad better than the next person's. If your ad is butting up right next to 10 other ads similar to yours, you want yours to stand out - of course because this brings you a lot more visitors.

Instead of just promoting your website, promote one specific thing on your website - pick the most valuable asset to your website, and promote that!

If it's a free e-book, advertise it. If it's a product, advertise it. If it's a professional video series, ADVERTISE IT.

You want to keep your ad short and to the point. Tell them who you are, what you are offering, and why it can help them/benefit them.

Like other traffic tactics, the more time you spend, the greater the reward. Post your ad to 1 site and get 100 visitors. Post it to 100 sites and get 10,000 visitors. Of course, you will get less visitors if your ad and offer are crap, and you can get much more if you have solid, converting ads and offers.

Run tests, see what works and what doesn't. I'm positive that by your 10th ad, you'll have the system down.

63

GET INVOLVED IN NICHE COMMUNITIES

Forums, blogs, masterminds, groups, these are all niche communities.

It's important to get involved in communities relevant to your site's content. Become known in these communities. Involve yourself in groups on Google+, Facebook, YouTube, and other social sites.

Niche communities help in many ways:

- When you post great content, you can tell your communities about it.

- When you need reviews and testimonials for a product, you can go to your communities and groups.

- When you want to team up, swap ads, or cross-promote, you can ask your communities.

Start communicating. Become friends with people. Have group discussions. It all helps with your business, branding, promotion, and of course, website traffic.

64

PLR Content "Can" Work Wonders

PLR stands for "private label rights".

In a nutshell, you basically create a piece of content (e-books are popular with PLR, and will be used in this strategy), and allow people to share it around for free. There is also an advanced strategy I'll teach you in this chapter as well.

First, you must create an e-book. You should already know how to do this - remember, it's easy!

But, in this e-book, you will make it clear that people can give your book away for free, either to their list, friends, family, post it on their website, ANYTHING they want. Also, you will include your website link (as many times as you want) in the e-book, and also make it clear that nothing is to be changed when giving the e-book away - you don't want people changing your website links to their own, or worse - promote a lousy product at the end of your e-book.

Then, use the same freebie/e-book distribution/traffic tactics that you used before. The more you promote, the more your book gets out there. The more it gets out there, the more people visit your website, and share your book with others.

Here's an advanced PLR strategy:

Do all of the same things as before, except instead of telling people they can give it away for free, tell them that they only way they can give this book to someone else is if they sell it (and yes, tell them that they make 100% profit!). You may think that this will bring you less traffic, and then people are making money with your free content, but with my experience, it can bring you more.

When people have the opportunity to make money for something they didn't create, and they make 100% profit, you better believe they will be promoting it like crazy! And when those people buy your book (from these other promoters/people), they now have the opportunity to make money promoting and selling your book.

And guess what? Through all this promotion and book buying (that you don't have to work on or worry about at all), your website link (and any other links in the book) will continue to be shown to more and more people.

You can change this tactic/add things, whatever you want - again, think outside the box. You can come up with your own great strategies - trust me, it's worth it.

65

Social Bookmarking

Remember StumbleUpon? That's just one of the more popular social bookmarking sites, there are hundreds of other great ones that can bring you lots of website traffic.

Social bookmarking allows people to "bookmark share" your website with the rest of the world - not only do they bookmark it for themselves, but it shows other people on the bookmark communities/websites as well, allowing others to bookmark (vote up/like/plus) your page or content.

Everyone has their own favorite social bookmarking sites, it's your job to be involved in all of them (or as many as you can without going crazy). The more you bookmark your content, pages, articles, and videos, and the more bookmarking sites you use, the more traffic your site can receive.

Just like with StumbleUpon, people love controversial, racy, funny, helpful, or life changing content. Make your content shine, bookmark it everywhere, and let others do the work.

What most people don't realize is the community aspect of social bookmarking sites. You can bookmark every single page of your site on 100 bookmarking sites, and although that will make your site rank higher in the search engines, you probably won't get much direct traffic from those bookmarks. The reason is simple: you have no following on these social bookmark sites.

On most social bookmarking sites, there are features that let you add or follow people, or join their bookmark community. Start "friending" or "following" people, whatever terminology they use, and gain a community of people that follow and see your bookmarks. This way, any time you bookmark a page on your site, these people will see your bookmark, and you'll start to see snowball effects of traffic when your best content drives up the rankings of social bookmarking sites, and then the search engines, and then the general public.

66

Create A Free Service

Remember this traffic tactic, because I hardly see anyone talking about it!

Free services are the most used and viewed websites online. I'm not saying it has to be as good as Facebook, but that's a good example of "free social networking". I'll get into other examples of free services in a bit.

The joy of having a free service on your website (especially if it's automated) is the fact that most people who use your service once and like it will use it again in the future, save it (bookmark), and share it with their following.

Now, you could either create a free service, or use someone else's free service. I'll explain both below, with examples for each.

Creating your own free service: If you know how to program basic web code, you can create free services that people can use online. Now, I'm guessing you don't have a bunch of skills with programming, so you may have to hire someone. You can hire someone to code a basic program to be used on your website for extremely cheap prices. Search online for outsourcing programming gigs, you'll find people who can code great services within hours, and you may only have to pay $50 - $100 for everything.

Using someone else's free service: If you can't create your own service, and you don't want to pay someone, you can always use someone else's for free. Many coders and programmers give out their source code, as well as full functioning plug-ins and services that you can plug right into your website with a simple Javascript or HTML code, and you can promote your website's service as if it were your own. You can get more traffic if you have many different services on your website.

There are many different types of services you can offer. I'll give a few examples below (some thought up by myself, and some I've seen before):

99 Ways To Flood Your Website With Traffic

- BPM (beat per minute) counter. This is great for DJs, producers, beat makers, and musicians. They simply go to the website, and start tapping the space bar on each beat to record the beats per minute. I checked the source code on this, and it could take a novice coder less than an hour to code.

- Back link creator. Everyone loves back links. Create a plug-in/program for your website that submits people's links to multiple websites (that you create yourself, all in different niches). All this takes is a few lines of code to set up, and you could have your very own back linking service.

- YouTube video looper. You've seen these. Easy to code? You bet! All it takes is a few lines of code, and the knowledge of YouTube's personal coding language (to set parameters for looping). There are dozens of sites that allow looping of YouTube videos. And these are services that people use all the time!

- Video/Website promotion. This was a business I used to have. I allowed people to submit their videos and websites through a simple form (1 minute set-up), and I would promote them using my own video view tactics. People loved it, and continued to visit my website daily.

These are just a few of the services and applications you can create and/or have created for you. You can decide to make the service it's own website, and then link to your other website at the top of the page, or you can just include the service right on your website (this is what I do - more traffic).

All you have to do is create some sort of service that saves people time, solves someone's problem, or helps someone, promote it using the other traffic tactics in this book, and as more people use your service, your traffic will continue to grow.

67
SCORE SOME INTERVIEWS

There's nothing better than an interview. With interviews, all you are doing is talking about yourself, your business, your website(s), what's going on right now (usually what you're selling), and what people can expect in the future.

Once you've had enough interviews, you'll start to notice the types of questions people ask, and they will get easier and easier. There's many different types of interviews you can score, and I'll list a handful of them below:

Radio Interviews - These are easier than you think. And contrary to popular belief, MOST radio is recorded. Sure, you may get the DJs and mix shows, and some occassional live shows, but they usually record these and then re-play them at a later time. So, you can score an interview with a radio station (email them, have others email them to tell them about you), go down to the station and record the interview with one of the DJs / MCs, and have it played multiple times in the future (also, don't forget online radio stations - sometimes online stations record weekly recordings with new interview spots every week - do your research!).

Newspaper Interviews - You'd be surprised at how many news reporters, writers, and columnists have NO story for tomorrow morning's paper. As they face a deadline, you could be their knight in shining armor. Email a handful of columnists and newspaper writers (most list their email addresses at the end of all their news articles), and tell them about yourself, your website, and tell them if they ever need a great interview, they can call you or email you. You can get some huge results if you email the right people, and many people.

Video Interviews - Video bloggers, "YouTubers", and other video creators and website would be happy to do a video interview with you. It's just more content for them, and brings a new face to their videos, which viewers tend to like. You can video chat your interview, or you can record the questions and answers separately, from different parts of the globe. Then, the video creator (with our mighty skills) will edit the interview and publish it to their websites/blogs/video channels.

99 Ways To Flood Your Website With Traffic

Blog Interviews - These are usually done by email. Go ahead and contact some blog owners, and tell them you would be happy for them to interview you on their website. Now, most of the time this should go the other way around (blog owners contact you), but if you know certain blogs that interview people with websites like you, you can surely contact them about an interview. They will usually respond with a set of questions, you write detailed answers, and they post the interview on their blog with your website link at the bottom of the post.

TV Interviews - I'll be honest, it's hard to score these, but I know people who have. Most of my buddies who have been interviewed on TV have told me their secret was press releases. They simply worded a few press releases as if they were a reporter talking about this "new great guy and website" (himself), and a few people who worked for popular TV networks saw it, emailed him, and he had 3 interviews within a week!

Yes, with interviews, you have to put yourself out there. If you don't like using your full name, or don't want the entire world to know that you own/operate your website, interviews aren't for you. But if you don't mind the publicity, and you can stand proud behind your website, then by all means, put yourself out there, and get some interviews.

68
Tell People To Share Your Blog, And Make It Easy!

Yep, the easiest way to get more traffic is to just tell people to share your blog.

There's a huge percentage of your visitors that would love to share your content, but it's not possible because you don't make it easy for them.

To make things easy, you should ALWAYS have a set of social/share buttons on each page of your site. If you are on a popular blog platform, you can find tons of plug-ins that work for any website.

Make sure to include the big social sites like Facebook, Twitter, and Google. Then, include popular social bookmarking sites (right now it's Reddit, StumbleUpon, and Digg). Finally, include a "bookmark" button, an "email this page" button, and any other popular sharing sites that have a good amount of traffic flowing to them.

Then, wherever you include these buttons, write some text above or below them saying something like "The best support I could ever ask for is for you to share this page!" - or "Sharing is caring", or something similar.

When you provide lots of options for sharing, and TELL people to share your blog, AND make it easy to share (1 click sharing), you'll get more and more people sharing your site. And when new traffic from these shares come rolling in, they'll see the same "sharing is caring" line with tons of social sharing buttons, and will be inclined to share your page, as their friends did just before.

69

WRITE BRANDABLE REPORTS AND SUBMIT EVERYWHERE

We talked about PDFs, free reports, and products. Now it's time to get into specific advanced strategies for e-books.

In this chapter, we are talking about brandable reports.

When you wrote your PDF before, you would include your website link at the beginning and end of the book. With a brandable report, you will "secretly" include your website links many times throughout the entire report.

First, you need LOTS of great content on your website, and it all must relate to eachother (as if when you put all the info together, it could form a relevant, flowing book).

If you already have a blog or site with lots of content on it (and it's all about the same core topic), then this is going to be easy for you.

Next, you create a short report (10 pages is fine, 20 is even better, no more than 30). Pack this e-book with valuable info, and really put your best stuff in the book. Reveal all, as I would say. Now, when you create your book, make sure each part of your book relates to a specific article on your website. Don't just re-write the article - but write something similar in the book. Then, at the end of this section, write a sentence like this: "If you want to know more about [sub-topic here], click here for an intersting article."

Now do this for all the sections of your book. You can make each section a half of a page to a page long, which could give you between 20 and 30 small sections that make up a book. Now, you can non-chalantly include links to your website, and people will just view them as EXTRA valuable content that they wouldn't otherwise have found if they hadn't read your free e-book.

Mick Macro

Submit it to e-book directories like you did before. Post it to your website. Share it around. Post it on freebie sites. Give it to friends. Share it on your list.

And of course, because your entire book is branded from top to bottom, you can entice and allow people to share your book for free with ANYONE they want, and continue to receive more traffic for each brandable report you publish.

70

Use "alt" in Images / Image Tags

This is something you may have heard before, but haven't used much at all - probably because you didn't see immediate results.

Well, using the "alt" tag in images on your website won't give you immediate traffic, but if have some great images and alt keywords, and have enough images on your site, you can begin to see increases in traffic. Here's why:

Many people search for images using Google images, and other similar image search engines. These images are found from the content found on the page that the picture is on, subtext that is right next to/underneath the image, and the "alt" tag in the image's details.

Just search "image alt html tag" or "img alt html", it's just one small line of code that you use to insert an image. If you insert images using a blog platform without code, they usually have an "alt text" box you can enter a keyword into.

You should use alt tags for all of your images. Some people write alt keywords that describe the image, but it's better to use the primary keyword for the article that the image shows on.

The key is having great images, and figuring out how to reverse engineer the searching process. What I mean is, if someone searches for "cool kickflip" in Google Images, and they see 100 images in front of them, what image will they click on? If you have a page talking about how to land a kick flip, and your site's main topic is skateboarding, and you have the coolest image of a kickflip with the alt tag set as "cool kickflip", you can be sure to get some traffic from Google Images.

Mick Macro

You may think that people will just click on the image, view it, decide if they want it, and then leave. However, I find that with great images and keywords that describe your page's content, more people will stop by your site to view the image their, because it is of their interest.

71

CONTINUE TO ENHANCE YOUR SITE

This should be a no-brainer, but most people don't like change, so enhancing their site isn't one of their main priorities. Make this a priority.

When I say "enhance your site", what I'm talking about is user-friendliness, navigation, design, features, services, color, images, and stuff like that.

Most people design their site ONCE, and then for the next 5 years, they just create content and promote their site. Then they find out they need to do major work on their site, and it's this big old re-launch process.

You should always continue to enhance your site. By doing this, you are showing your visitors you care, and that you have their best interest in mind. When you create new features and services, better navigation, and more sharing options, you wil in turn have more happy visitors (and happy visitors means happy website owners!).

Here's some easy ways to continue to enhance your website or blog:

- Make navigation easy. Only put your main pages in your navigation. Home, Blog, About, Contact, Service 1, Service 2, Member's Club (maybe other pages, but not much more than this!). Give them too many things to choose, and they'll just get mad and leave.

- Go to your homepage. What are the first few things you notice on your homepage? If you were a visitor of your site, what catches your eye first. This strategy I'm about to share with you has helped my website grow beyond any other strategy, listen to these next few sentences: Whenever I feel like enhancing my site, I put my computer in front of a family member or friend, and open my homepage. I tell them, "Navigate around my site like you were interested, and keep going to different pages without leaving the site." By doing this, I get to see what they click on first, if they get stuck anywhere, what pages are they on when they click back to the homepage because nothing is there? Are their any links or buttons that NO ONE clicks? All of this helps your site beyond belief, and you will start to notice things you didn't previously notice.

- Copy other sites. Okay, don't directly copy their code, but take certain design features of their sites, and implement the same types of design in your site. What features do these sites have that you don't have? What more could you bring to the table on your website? Try to be better than your competitors, always taking your site one step further. You'll start to see yourself passing up one competitor after another (in terms of traffic and site rank).

The point is, the more you make your site better (navigation, ease-of-use, design, content), the more your visitors will love you for it. And your visitors always come before robots, spiders, and search engines. When you have the social proof of people loving your website, the robot spiders and Google penguins and pandas will take notice (haha, I love these terms, Google has an entire barnyard of updates).

72
PUBLISH A MINI-COURSE

A mini-course is easy because you create it once, and put it on autopilot immediately. Then, you never have to touch it again, and it will continue to generate tons of traffic to your website.

We talked about email lists and autoresponders. A mini-course is the best type of email autoresponder set-up you could have. Here's how it works:

You create a set of emails, where each email takes someone one step further to a desired goal. You plug these in to your autoresponder. If you have 7 emails, that means you have a 7 day mini-course. Write all 7 emails for the mini-course, and set them up so that each one sends one day after the previous one.

Make sure each email includes a link to your website. Also, if you have extra content that goes along with your email for a specific day, you can link to a page, article, or video on your website from each email.

Now all that is left is adding your opt-in box to your website. You can create a new page and call it "7 Day Mini-Course For [Topic Here]" - also make sure you list bullet points of what your email subscribers can expect to learn or benefit from this e-course.

Once your course is out there, it's time to promote. You know about promotion, you just read about 71 different strategies for promotion! I know you can generate 10s of thousands of visitors to this e-course page - SO DO IT!

Because once you start promoting it, it starts to promote itself. More people share it, comment about it, talk about it.

This helps you in a few different ways. First, each mini-course member will essentially see your website link up to 14 or more times throughout the e-course, so you are bound to get many views from each subscriber. Next, you are now building a huge email list where you can promote your website to in the future, or promote your other "exclusive tips" or "member's list" to. You can also promote and make money from other people's products using your list.

The possibilities are endless. You can even combine strategies. For each day of your e-course, giveaway a brandable e-book, and allow people to sell it (PLR). Give away freebies, entice people to share your other content. When you start to combine strategies and allow things to work with eachother, you can literally FLOOD your website with traffic (there, I said the title of the book!).

73
PARTICIPATE IN GROUPS

I'll keep this chapter brief, as you've already learned about joining communities.

Instead of talking about communities in general again, let's talk about social networking groups. These are not forums or groups of websites, these are usually smaller groups of people that have formed or joined a group within a social network (like a Facebook Group, or a Google+ Circle Group, etc.)

When you join groups like this, you start to have a sort of brand that goes along with you. When I made beats, I joined tons of facebook groups for beat makers, musicians, and music promoters. I would post my beats, took a lot of criticism, but ended up getting lots of visitors, and making lots of contacts.

And that's what these groups are all about - making contacts. You shouldn't always be worried about instant traffic (although instant is a good feeling). Form relationships with other like-minded people, and it can go a long way. Who would have known that some "tech" guy I met in a Facebook group would go on to be a business partner of mine in a co-op product we created together. He did all the tech stuff, while I had the creative side of it.

Make friends, keep in contact with people, prove yourself as an expert in your field, and you'll have followers of like-minded people - people who will be your main partners, affiliates, members, and visitors of your website (and buyers of your products once you create some!).

74

BE THE FIRST COMMENTER ON OTHER BLOGS

This chapter builds on the blog commenting strategy you learned previously.

With blog commenting (especially blogs that offer DoFollow back links), you can generate tons of great back links for your website, and receive thousands of visitors for just a handful of useful blog comments.

Now it's time to kick things up a notch.

I'm actually going to talk about two different strategies. I didn't want to name the chapter as both of these strategies, as one only works if it is enabled on the blog you are commenting on.

The first strategy is being the first commenter on blogs. Usually, blogs will display the first comments at the top, giving you prime real estate on their website. If you can write the first comment on a popular blog, this is the first thing that visitors will see after reading the article.

It's easiest to be the first commenter if you do two things. First, you must join their email list, as bloggers always send their articles to their email list first (usually). Next, you have to always have your email account open and handy, so when you get the email, you can rush to the post to write the first comment.

DON'T WRITE A LOWSY COMMENT - IT WILL BE DELETED. Most bloggers know that the first comment is prime positioning for a website back link. Don't write lowsy comments on these blogs, or they can delete your comment, and even ban you from future commenting on their entire blog! Read the whole post, write a thoughtful comment, and show that you read the entire article.

99 Ways To Flood Your Website With Traffic

The second strategy is being the top commenter on blogs. Now, I've only seen a handful of blogs implement this feature in their comments. Usually blogs will have to use an external comment plug-in for features like this. But basically, this comes down to the value of the content in the comment. Even if you are the 100th comment, if you can write the best comment on that post, people with +1 it, thumbs it up, like it (whatever), and you could find yourself at the top of the list.

This works even better because there is already social proof that shows that you know what you are talking about. Most comments that have social proof like this will evoke interest in people, and they will click on your linked name to visit your website to find out more about you.

75

Post About Current Events

This strategy is all about posting about current events, or what I like to call, media jacking.

Before I tell you the strategy, let me tell you this: Don't piggyback on EVERY single news story out there, only ones that relate to your website in some sort of way.

Okay, on to the details:

Media jacking works like this... Watch TV, listen to the radio (TV is better), and wait around for "breaking news" stories.

When "breaking news" happens, listen up. Find out if it has something to do with your site. When the news comes on, listen to see what stories they will be talking about "tonight at 5", or "tonight at 10", whenever.

If any of the topics has anything to do with the content on your site, you will definitely be writing an article immediately.

For example: If you have a dog training site, and a news story comes on about a "talking dog", you are going to write about a talking dog tonight.

Let's take the talking dog example further...

When the news about this magical dog comes on, take notes. Write down the dog's name, the title of the news story, the name of the owner, the city where they live, and any other important details used in the story. Try to reverse-engineer things again. If you saw this story, and wanted to know more, what would you search for online? Title your article accordingly, and include all the main keywords used in the news story.

99 Ways To Flood Your Website With Traffic

The key to this strategy is timing. You MUST be first. As soon as the breaking news hits the television, START WRITING. Write everything you can about this talking dog. Find YouTube videos of "talking dogs", and embed them in your post, and write about those. Write a HUGE article, spend lots of time on it, and sprinkle the keywords from the story throughout the entire page.

Publish, quick quick quick! You want your article/content published on your website within an hour of the story going live. It's better if it's within minutes - yes, this is a wild and crazy process.

Once your article is published, go into MAXIMUM SHARING MODE. Share the story around, show search engines that you are SET on these new keywords. Ping your article. Now, because this is a brand new story, it's likely that these keywords and keyword phrases you used haven't been used by any others (take for instance, "talking dog miloh from ohio").

Now is where you sit back and let the magic happen. People will start searching for these keywords (the ones you already researched quickly and published before anyone else), and guess who's article shows up first in the search engines? That's right, YOURS!

If half a million people saw the news story, and 1% (5,000 people) search for it in the first few hours, you could have thousands of visitors flowing to your website. And since your website is about dog training, and these people want to see a talking dog, they are already pre-sold and interested in the content you have on your website. So if you have other traffic tactics in place, you could pump your website to the max within hours.

76

Build Other Websites and Blogs and Link

Remember Squidoo and Hubpages, where you created articles, hubs, lenses, and other pages that have content that links to your website?

This strategy is built sort of the same way, but instead of posting these pages to one account on one site, you are creating whole new blogs and sites, and linking to your main website from it.

Now, you may be thinking, "I'm still working on my first website, I can't even imagine trying to handle more..." However, this is much easier than you think.

Traffic strategy #21 was blogger blogs and free blog sites. This strategy works the same way, except I want you to now create new domains (it will only cost $10 - $15 for each added domain).

When you link to your site from free blogger and wordpress sites/blogs, you will get traffic, but it's better to have back links on primary domains (so instead of site.wordpress.com or site.blogger.com, it would be site.com).

Get a few domains (choose your domain names based on keywords you want to rank for), write a few pages of content on the site, and link to your primary site many times on each domain. Search engines will view this as an external (someone else's) keyworded domain/site linking to your site, and they will rank you for these new keywords, and rank you higher in general because of these new backlinks.

If you don't want to buy new sites, and want to go the free route, here's another strategy:

You can go for a site.blogger.com free site, but instead of just blogging, and having to update the site sometimes, create a static website with one primary piece of content/freebie/video/service. Find ways to interlink these websites to your primary website. If it's one long report on a one page site, link to your primary site inside the content, and at the end of the page. If it's a video, make sure you mention your site or link to it below the video. If you are giving away a freebie, make sure your freebie links to your website.

The more external websites, URLs, and domains that link to your website, the higher your website will rank (especially if the site's content relates to yours closely), and the more visitors you will get.

77

EVERY TIME YOU PUBLISH CONTENT, SHARE IT EVERYWHERE

This chapter marks the end of the "free traffic strategies" section of this book, and I saved the best for last.

This strategy ties all 76 previous strategies together into one.

It's simple: Every time you publish content, share it everywhere.

You have the share buttons on your site. You have an email list. You've joined tons of social networks. You have twitter followers and facebook fans, and are gaining every day. You have video sharing site accounts. You have ping sites saved, and a big list of directories. You have lists of freebie sites, and know how to write brandable e-books.

When you have 100s of different traffic strategies, and all of them intertwine with eachother somehow, you create an auto-pilot traffic system that works on it's own.

The more you work on these strategies, the easier it is to get the whole world to see it.

So, whenever you publish a piece of content, share it everywhere. Pick your favorite traffic strategies, and put them in a list (with links to all the websites and services you will use). Each time you publish content, go down your list, checking off each traffic strategy as you implement it.

It could go something like this:

99 Ways To Flood Your Website With Traffic

- Publish content.

- Ping this page using [this ping service].

- Share this on the 5 social networks I am a part of.

- Post a link to the 10 groups I am a part of.

- Send an email to my 4,398 email subscribers.

- Social bookmark the content using [these 20 social bookmarking sites].

- Add this page into my traffic exchange rotation, and generate 5,000 views/visitors on it.

- Write external content on my 3 external blogs, 1 squidoo lens, and 2 hub pages.

- Add this link to your forum signature for a few days.

- This list could go on forever, but you get the idea.

The bigger your following, the better your content, and the more you share it, the more visitors and higher site rank you will have.

Paid Sources of Traffic

You have more than enough strategies for generating free traffic, now it's time for PAID TRAFFIC.

Although you can get lots of traffic for free, it often takes lots of work - paying for traffic makes it easy to get as many visitors as you want pouring in to your website at any given moment.

I always suggest starting with free traffic first. Also, before paying for any type of traffic, make sure you either a) have a larger budget OR b) can monetize that traffic and make your investment back with ease.

You can get all the traffic in the world, but unless that traffic is targeted, and you have monetization strategies in place, that traffic means nothing, as you will have to pay for this traffic (hosting fees, email list fees, etc.)

With that said, let's get into some paid traffic sources.

78

Expired Domain Traffic

If you want to make small, SMART investments, and don't have a huge budget, expired domain traffic is for you.

This one is a fun strategy for those who hardly have any budget for advertising, and can work wonders if you know how to use it correctly.

Here's how expired domain traffic works:

People buy domain names. Maybe they even build a website on that domain name. They start to get thousands of visitors each month. Maybe they lose interest in the site, maybe they don't care about the site anymore, or maybe they just forgot to pay their domain re-registration bill.

Whatever the reason is, domain names expire all the time. Some of these domains that expire still get tons of visitors, and these visitors are just led to a basic site landing page - those one's that people click the BACK button on because it's an auto-generated link list and advertisements that the domain companies make money from.

There are also websites out there that specialize in telling you all of the popular domain names that are about to expire. I've seen recently expired domain names that still get over 10,000 visitors per day!

When these domain names expire, they basically go "up for grabs" to the first buyer. And since these domains aren't being sold by the website owner, they are usually only $10 or $15.

Almost ANY expired domain is worth the $15 investment. Let's say an expired domain gets 20,000 visitors per month. That's 240,000 visitors per year! By investing $15 for one year of this domain, and then re-directing the domain (the domain company you get the domain with can do this for you in one click) to your own website, you

Mick Macro

are spending just $15 for 240,000 website visitors!

If you brake this down, that's $1 for every 16,000 visitors to your website! I bet you could make a lot more than $1 for 16,000 visitors.

And the funny thing is, there are plenty of expired domains that get much more traffic than this!

The only reason people don't use this tactic is because they are too lazy, and don't want to spend the 10 minutes it takes to buy a new domain, spend $15, and click one button to re-direct this domain to their own website.

One more tip for expired domain buying: It's better if you buy expired domains that have keywords related to your website, or at least make sure the website that existed on the domain previously relates to yours. You don't want to re-direct CoolGardeningSite.com to your site if it's about break dancing.

79

PAY PER CLICK ADVERTISING

Pay per click advertising is one of the most basic forms of traffic generation and advertising, and has been around for a very long time.

Google Adwords/Adsense = Pay Per Click Advertising.

PPC Advertising works like this: You and others bid on keywords, and the highest bidder gets the top spot on websites and in search results (in the ad areas). When someone clicks on your ad, you pay the bid you requested. Bid too high, and waste your money. Bid too low, and you'll never have your ad shown, because others are bidding higher than you all the time.

Although PPC advertising works great for bringing in the highest-targeted traffic you can find, I don't recommend it for newbies.

PPC advertising can be expensive. If you bid on a keyword for $1 per click, you'll have to pay $100 for 100 visitors. Out of these 100 visitors, you'll have to monetize your site enough to make more than $100 to get your investment back (and unless you are selling an expensive product and get lucky, you probably won't make back your initial investment).

If you have something for sale on your site, and word your advertisement accordingly, you CAN do okay. However, if you are just looking to increase your website traffic only, there are other traffic strategies other than this one that can work better for you.

80
Cost Per View Advertising

Cost per view, or CPV advertising is something that many people still don't know about. It's not new in any way, it just hasn't seemed to hit the PPC level of popularity.

With CPV advertising, you can pay just pennies for visitors (compared to DOLLARS for PPC ads). I've seen CPV ads run for $0.01 (yes, one cent!) per visitor, and many that run at $0.02 - $0.05 per visitor (these are still amazing rates compared to most other advertising strategies).

The reason some CPV companies are so cheap is because they are able to control their ad system in entirety.

Most CPV networks are owned by companies that produce/publish "website bars" (like "hotbar"), where users of the bar are able to get premium downloads, videos, screensavers, desktop images, icons, and more for FREE.

In return for getting this free premium "stuff", the user agrees that the company can show them advertisements while they browse the web.

Basically, you bid on keywords AND URLs, and once someone searches for the keyword you bid on, or once someone visits the URL you chose, instead of seeing search results or the website they requested, they are shown YOUR website (and you pay $0.01 or $0.02 for this visitor).

The key is bidding low on everything (I always go for minimum bid), and bidding only on specific URLs that are relevant to your website. This is great for stealing visitors from competitors. If you have are a musician, and your competitor (another musician) gets millions of visitors to their website, you can bid on their URL, so everytime someone (who has the web bar installed and has agreed to see advertisements) goes to view that musician, they are taken to YOU instead.

99 Ways To Flood Your Website With Traffic

At $0.02 per visitor, you can spend $100 and get 5,000 visitors seeing your site. Let's say they searched your bidded keyword "buy professional beats online". Instead of seeing search results, they see your website where you sell your beats. If you spent $100 to get 5,000 people wanting to buy beats to come to your website, and you sell each beat for $100 or more, all you have to do is sell just one beat to one of those 5,000 people to make your investment back (and even if you don't, you should be collecting their email addresses using an opt-in form, and have other sharing options/buttons on your site to extend your traffic - it's like getting more traffic for the money you spent).

81

Pay Per Month Ads

Pay per month ads do take a bigger initial investment, but can work well if you know what types of ad spots to buy.

There are hundreds of sites that allow people to buy and sell ad spots on their website for a specific set amount of time (most of the time, people set the duration at 30 days, or one month).

Now, too many sites charge way too much for ad space on their site. I've seen some sites that only get 10,000 visitors per month charge $50 for a month for one small ad that sits next to 6 other ads just like it. Don't get caught up with stuff like this. Do the math. $50 for 10,000 visitors TIMES .5% or less clicking on your ad = 50 visitors (and you don't want to and shouldn't ever pay $50 for 50 visitors).

However, you can always find a few gems for advertising deals. These are the people who either can't get $50 for an ad spot, or just price their rate low so they can fill all their spots.

Browse through the different sites offering ads. You are looking for the diamond in the rough. You are looking for that site that gets 100,000 visitors per month offering a prime ad spot for $20 per month (that's $1 for each 5,000 ad views).

There are 3 ways you can get a higher click through rate on your ad:

1. Make a better ad. It doesn't even have to look professional. My best performing ads are completely red bold text on a white background.

2. Chose prime ad spots. Don't go for the 125x125 square sidebar ad next to 8 other ads. Go for the ad right above the content, away from all the other fuss.

3. Choose more relevant sites. Again, you can't advertise a music site on a gardening site. You will get 0 clicks and waste your money. Find the most relevant websites to yours. Just think, "If I was on this site, and I saw an ad for my site, would I be interested?"

In order to succeed with pay per month ads, you need to make sure all of the little details are perfectly set in stone. This isn't PPC where you can change your ad 10 times in the same day. Once you buy your "banner spot" and submit your ad, you can only change it by waiting the duration of the ad, and then purchasing the same spot again with a different ad.

82

Facebook Advertising

Some people like to think of it like "Google is good at keyword marketing, Facebook is good at people marketing".

The great aspect that facebook brings to advertising is the targeting options and social proof.

You can target specific groups of people, geographically, and many other targeting parameters. On top of that, you can buy an ad spot that shows someone's friends when they "facebook like" your website.

I can't tell you all the ins and outs of advertising on facebook, as I've seen it change all the time, and what I say about specifics won't matter in a few months. However, I can tell you that when used correctly, you can get visitors for pennies.

My super-tip for advertising on facebook: Whether you are leading your click-through visitors to a facebook landing page or your website (external domain), make sure you have a clear call-to-action on your page.

Get them to download a freebie. Get them to buy a product. Get them to join your e-mail list. Get them to share your website. Get them to like your facebook page and follow you on twitter.

Have one or a few clear CTAs on the page, and get rid of all the other clutter. If you know how to make a splash page (just a tiny page with a headline, some sub-text, and an e-mail list or CTA), that works even better. But if it's just a regular page on your website, that's okay too, just keep things clear and to-the-point.

Form your advertisement with your CTA in mind. "Like us on facebook", "Buy this product", "Join this club free", "Get this freebie". Of course, you want to add at least a couple more details in your ad - don't just say "get this freebie" - I think you get the idea though.

99 Ways To Flood Your Website With Traffic

To get better at facebook advertising, take a look at how others are doing it. Follow the experts - not the "gurus", but the actual dudes who know what they are talking about. Don't throw $100 down the drain if you are just starting with Facebook advertising. Start with a $5 or $10 per day budget, test some ads, and work your way up from there.

83

VIDEO ADVERTISING

If you know how to make a simple promotional video for your website, video advertising can be fun and rewarding. Even if you don't know how to make a video ad, you can hire someone for EXTREMELY CHEAP to create one for you.

First, let me tell you about two different types of video advertising (in my mind, these are the top 2 you should focus on):

1. YouTube Video Promos - I'm not talking about basic video advertising on YouTube (that is included in #2 below), I'm talking about creating a video or channel on YouTube, and then promoting it via YouTube pre-roll video advertising.

   For this type of ad, you focus on creating a promotional video for your website, and post it to YouTube. Then, you use promo pre-roll ads to play part of your video, and they can decide to click to view your video. I'll also include that you can pay for video promotions by buying a "sponsored video spot" on YouTube.

   You pay when someone views your video (check YouTube for payment specifics). The more views you get (the more you pay), the bigger the snowball effect when your video continues to rise in views after the initial promotion (and if your promo is good, you'll get lots of website visitors).

2. Regular Video Ads - This type covers all other video ads, on all sites including YouTube. This is where you create a 30 second, or 15 second, or 60 second video ad/commercial for your website, and pay for views or clicks depending on the company serving the ads.

No matter what type of video advertising you use, you should always have a great video ad - and if you can't make it super-professional, at least make it shocking, or crazy, or controversial, or so weird and intersting that people are curious and click.

99 Ways To Flood Your Website With Traffic

Or... you could outsource your video ad to someone for "little moneys" as my nephew likes to call it.

My favorite site for outsourcing little gigs like this is Fiverr (I've already seen other sites come out similar to Fiverr, so you can bet if Fiverr isn't around, some other website just like it is). In a nutshell, Fiverr works like this: People list things they will do for $5, and you choose the gig, pay the $5, Fiverr keeps the $5 until the gig is completed, then you mark it complete, then the person gets their $5.

Sometimes, fiverr sellers will list "bonuses" or "add ons", where for 5 more dollars, or 10 more dollars, or even 20 more dollars, you can get extra perks attached to your gig.

For example, if someone was going to do a 30 second audio commercial ad spot for $5, they might say "for 5 more dollars, I'll do 90 seconds!". If someone was creating a video advertisement (in our case) where they create a professional 30 second simple ad, they might ad $10 or $20 bonuses where they will add professional music, or pro editing, or extra branding features.

Search around on Fiverr and other sites like this. Look at the seller's ratings and reviews. If someone has an amazing video ad gig that will only cost you $10, and they have great reviews and 100% feedback rating, GET THE GIG.

84
Pop-Up Advertising

Pop-up advertising can be very cheap, and also brings great results when used the right way.

There are 2 main strategies for pop-up advertising. I'll explain both below:

1. Adware/web bar pop-ups: These work like the CPV ads explained in chapter 80. You pay per visitor/view, and these pop-ups are displayed to people who opted-in to advertising when they installed some sort of web bar or software.

With these types of popups, you can literally bid on any keyword, and any site you want. This is my favorite type of pop-up advertising.

2. Ad network pop-ups: With ad network pop-ups, you must first join an ad network that can display your advertisement as a pop-up.

The reason these differ from adware pop-ups is they will only show up on websites that have a specific code on their site to show the pop-ups. These are websites that are fine with showing pop-ups on their site. The reason I stay away from these and go for adware pop-ups is simple: If someone browses on a site that continuously shows pop-up ads, when mine is shown on one of these sites, it will be easily ignored and Xed out of.

On the other hand, with adware pop-ups, I can bid on any website URL, and any keyword. I can bid on ebay.com if I wanted to (pun intended), and because people aren't used to seeing pop-ups on ebay, they are more likely to take a quick glance at what this pop-up says. So if the site you bid on is super-relevant to your site, people may just click on your pop-up and start browsing around on your site instead.

85
Pop-Under Advertising

This is going to be another one of those brief chapters, only because I don't want to bore you with the same stuff. I'd rather tell you what you need to know, and if you already know something (from reading it earlier in the book), then I expect you to know about it and what it means.

So with that said, pop-under advertising is similar to pop-up and CPV advertising. You can use it the same two ways (adware/web bar, and ad networks), and the only difference is your ad is shown below or "under" (hence the name "pop-under") the site you bidded on (or the site that shows your ad).

Pop-under ads usually run for lower prices than pop-ups for the obvious reason. People aren't shown the site immediately, but instead once they leave the site (and sometimes not until hours later when they close their browser and find out a window has been open under their browser the entire time!).

Pop-unders work well if you change your thinking on advertising a little. With pop-ups, you want people to immediately do something. They are looking for answers, entertainment, news, and they want it NOW. With pop-unders, you have to think like the person viewing your ad. Your music ad may have shown up 20 minutes ago when they were viewing a music site, but now they are on wikipedia researching for a paper! And when they go to close their browser, they see your music ad! So instead of advertising it like "GO DO THIS NOW!", advertise it like, "Did you find what you were looking for?" - because chances are they didn't. That's why they left in the first place, so of course their going to answer "no...", and click through to your website "for a quick minute" before they shut down their computer.

I'll say it again, try to reverse-engineer everything. Think like the person being advertised to. When are they seeing your ad? Where are they seeing it? Are they buyers or freebie seekers? Do they make enough money to be able to even buy your product? Are they interested in your website or offer?

Mick Macro

These are all things you need to think about when using different types of advertising and traffic strategies.

86

Interstitial Ads

Interstitial ads are similar to pop-up, pop-under, and CPV, but differ in many different ways as well.

- With CPV/adware ads, the visitor gets redirected straight to your website.

- With pop-up ads, the visitor is shown your ad immediately (on top of the website they were going to).

- With pop-under ads, the visitor is shown your ad below all other windows, usually causing them to view your offer later.

With interstitial ads, your website/advertisement is shown for a set duration (usually something like 5 or 10 seconds) as a bar at the top of your site counts down to 0. Then, the viewer has the choice to "skip this and continue to site", or they can just keep browsing around your site (in which the countdown interstitial bar disappears).

It's hard to say if you can make a lot of money with these, but you can definitely get website traffic using interstitials!

It's all about what types of websites use interstitials, and also the relevancy of your website to the page this person wants to get to. Even if your site is about music (but specifically music producers and beat makers), if someone really wants to buy a saxophone, they'll skip your ad completely. However, even if they skip your ad, it still counts as a unique website visitor, as your page does indeed load.

87

Newspaper Ad Buying

These next 3 (newspaper ads, radio ads, and TV ads) are similar to the "free interviews" that I talked about earlier in the book, however instead of working non-stop to score a free interview, you are instead paying for an ad spot (which does cost money, but is easier and faster).

First up is newspaper ad buying. There are two ways you can go about this:

1. Solo Newspaper Ad Buying - This is where you pick one specific newspaper (sometimes a group of a few) to advertise in for a set duration (one paper, one week of papers, etc.).

If you have a low budget, this is where to start. Make your ad stand out, and think about the people you are advertising to. Where are you located? Your ad should sound different in th New York Times than it does in the Timbuktu Daily (I don't know if that exists).

2. Newspaper Circulation Buying - There are a few different sites/services online that allow you to post your advertisement to hundreds and thousands of newspapers across the globe for one fee (for each ad).

Do a search for "newspaper ad buying" or "mass newspaper ads". Find a service that can give you the most for your money. The reason I say this is because these packages tend to get expensive. Sure, you can get your ad in front of 5 million people, but it might cost you a few hundred dollars - so this type of mass newspaper ad buying might not be for you if you are on a low advertising budget.

One more thing I'll say about newspaper ads: Don't run a newspaper ad until you see success with in ONLINE. Once an ad is successful online, you can then start to test it offline the same way you did on the internet. Test test test, then when it's working, SCALE UP.

88

Radio Spots / Ads

Again, there are two ways to do these ads: Contact local radio stations, or use an online service to play your ad to tons of different radio stations.

I tend to like to do local radio stations, mainly because I like to hear my ad on the radio (I'm not that egotistic though, trust me - I just like to make sure I'm getting premium service for my money spent).

With radio ads, I encourage you to hire a voice actor. Again, Fiverr (and similar sites) - most can do a basic 30 second radio ad for $5, and then include uncopyrighted music for $5 more. So you may spend $10 - $20 on the creation of the ad, and then anywhere from $25 - $100s or $1,000s for the actual radio ad spot.

The reason I always hire voice actors is because of two things:

1. I'm no professional. I don't have that "radio voice". If I were to record my own audio/radio ad spot, I probably wouldn't be able to get anyone interested in what I have to offer.

2. Most radio stations won't accept lousy or unprofessional sounding ads. If there are scratches, or the treble is too high, or if you sound distorted, or even if they can't hear you - it doesn't really matter the reason, they can reject you 100 times quicker than it took you to make the ad.

Don't make that mistake. Hire someone who does it for a living - make it sound perfect. Some people on Fiverr (and other similar sites) might even form the entire radio ad for you with no script! - although you may have to include some basic details and a call-to-action for your ad.

89

TV Advertising

Did you know you can buy TV ad spots online nowadays?

I've never done a TV ad, but my friends have - they have mixed feelings. Sometimes it's hard to get website traffic from a TV ad, because it usually requires someone either having their phone or computer handy to visit your site immediately, or it requires them to memorize your website/domain name.

But nonetheless, they do claim they saw a slight increase in visitors. Usually you have to pay a lot for these ad spots. However, you can pay MUCH MUCH less if you go for less popular networks/channels and late night instead of prime time. Prime time ad space can cost thousands, and for super-prime-time (like when 1 million viewers are planned), you can expect to pay 10s of thousands.

But, for super late night less popular networks, you can have budgets of $10 - $50 per day, and only pay when your ad is shown.

Again, you will probably need to hire a professional in order to get this done correctly. Fiverr, ELance, and other outsourcing sites are great for stuff like this.

Bottom line: If you are just starting out with paid advertising, don't start with TV ads. Only go with TV ads once you have a team of people that can put together a professional commercial, as well as when you have a bigger budget to spend on more powerful advertising tactics.

90
BUY TEXT LINKS

Text link ads are basically text link spots (basic back links) that you buy in order to have your website link in a determined area of someone's website.

These are great for two reasons:

First, you get direct website traffic from someone clicking on a text link. It doesn't look like an ad, just another link on someone's website.

Second, this is considered a "back link" in the minds of the search engines, so your website will be ranked accordingly (score some text links on high page ranked sites and watch your rank get higher as well).

Some websites allow you to buy links directly on their website. Their are also "text link broker" sites that act as the middle man when buying and selling text link ads.

Sites like these make it easier to buy text links, because it is all automated, and you don't have to worry about anything being screwed up. Instead of the website owner having to edit the text link themselves, they just keep the same code on their site that displays the text links, and the broker site takes care of duration of the text link, which ones to rotate, etc.

Look around, and find some text link broker sites that have good deals. Remember, even if you don't get direct traffic, a back link is always great no matter what.

91

SOCIAL MEDIA BUYING

This is one of my favorite paid advertising techniques, but not for the ROI (return on investment), but because of the social proof it brings to my brands and businesses.

When I say social media buying, I mean buying twitter followers, buying YouTube subscribers/views, buying facebook likes/fans.

As long as popular social networking sites exist, there will always be sites that offer to sell you whatever type of "currency" is offered on each site (followers, fans, +1s, shares, links, posts, pins, you name it!).

Before going ahead with any social media buys, make sure you research for at least an hour or two. Put together lists of dozens of different companies you research. Write down their prices. Sometimes, people just go for the lowest price. But if 1 guy offers 1,000 twitter followers for $1, and most other services offer 1,000 twitter followers for $15 - $30, you might wonder what type of cheap system that other guy runs.

Now, social media buying always starts controversy. Some say "you shouldn't be able to buy followers/fans/likes - it's like buying people's attention if you have enough money". And my response to them is, "so is advertising".

That's how you have to look at this stuff. You shouldn't keep buying YouTube subscribers until you have 100,000 subscribers and then brag about it. But, there's no doubt in my mind that if you buy your way to that many subscribers, it's easier to gain larger amounts in the future because of the added exposure lots of subscribers brings.

It's all about social proof. Show the people of these social networks and websites that you and your website are important! Remember, it's easier for a snowball to roll if it's already large and has momentum.

92
FORUM ADVERTISING

When people go to pay for advertising, most go the normal route - advertise in search results, on blogs, on websites.

Let me take you out of your comfort zone, and introduce you to forum advertising. Now, when I say "forum advertising", it just means "some sort of" advertising on a forum. Each forum will have different types of ads - cost per month, CPC, CPV, CPM, etc.

In order to make this work, you have to do some math again.

Figure out how much it will cost you per month, per week, per click, per view, etc. for each advertising package. If you find out you are paying $100 to get your ad viewed only 10,000 times, that's $1 per 100 ad views, which if 1% click on it, means $1 per visitor.

However, if you search around for the right forum advertising package, you could get a package like $25 for a full month of advertising - and then you find out your ad will get an estimated 500,000 views! That's $1 for 20,000 ad views, and if 1% click on it, that means $1 per 8 visitors. The higher your percentage of clicks, the more visitors you can get. This all comes with having a great advertisement and offer, and promoting it to the right people.

Just do your research, don't spend too much money upfront, and always expect the worst - that you will get 0 visitors from your efforts. Learn from your mistakes, and do better next time. Eventually, all of this will come easy to you (I was once a newbie, we all were).

93

BUYING FIVERR GIGS

I've mentioned Fiverr a few times in previous chapters - now it gets it's OWN chapter!

I just want to talk a little about how to use Fiverr, as well as outsourcing in general.

If you are new to outsourcing, Fiverr is a good start, because you can start with just $5. I remember after purchasing large advertising sums for years, I found Fiverr, and just to test out gigs to see how they did, I spent $50 on 10 different gigs. I can honestly tell you that it was worth every penny.

It's all about feedback, reviews, and gig ratings. If the seller has 100% (or close to it) rating, with nothing but great feedback and reviews, it's probably safe to say that the gig is okay to buy.

Don't buy unneccessary gigs:

We all fall into buying unneccessary things. Especially when they are priced low. It's easy to spend "just another $5", but then you find out that 20 of these "$5s" is $100. It adds up, make sure you are spending it wisely.

Don't buy e-books on Fiverr. If they are selling it for $5, chances are it's either a short re-branded report, or even worse, an affiliate promotion. Of course, there are always exceptions - there's some good e-books on Fiverr, but it's unneccessary since right now you are focusing on direct website traffic.

Go for social networking/bookmarking/sharing gigs. Website traffic gigs are great. Same goes for back links, link wheels, and professional SEO link pyramids (and pro SEO work in general).

Go browse through some Fiverr gigs. Don't get lost, you could be there for awhile, gig-browsing is addicting.

94

Paid Blog Post

Yep, you can pay people to post your article to their blog (with all links intact - considering you follow their link and quality rules).

"Pay per post" type sites help out with this. They match bloggers with content advertisers in order for bloggers to make money and advertisers get more website traffic (or to pay for a product, join a list, etc.).

With paid blog posts, you are essentially paying someone to advertise your site/blog/service in a way that doesn't look like an advertisement at all. Everyone wins with paid blog posts.

Some blogs may require you to provide an entire blog post, and they will just submit it to their site. Other blogs will make it their own service to write the post for you (this usually costs more, so start with writing it yourself).

I find the average paid blog post costs anywhere from $10 - $20. But don't quote me on that, that's just the average of what I've seen over the years. Trust me, you can find people who will post your stuff for $1 (although I don't recommend going that cheap, as it's probably a super-low quality site). I've paid $5 plenty of times for paid blog posts that brought in a few hundred visitors each. I've also paid $50 for a blog post on a popular website, and got 30,000 website visitors in one day (which in my case, ended up in some quick cash from a product I was promoting).

For penny pinchers, buy a handful of dollar posts. Sometimes these work better than you think - but when you have more money to spend, score some posts on some more popular blogs.

95

Paid Press Releases

If you remember, you learned about free press releases in chapter 33.

You know that your press release should be short and sweet and to the point. It should have a clear call to action, and should be announcing something BIG.

So if you can do a free press release, why go for a paid press release?

Paid press releases are good because they reach a bigger scale than free PRs. Often, paid press release sites have a bigger distrubution team, bigger partners, and can basically get your PR in front of the eyes of popular magazines, newspapers, and other media outlets.

In a nutshell, paid press releases help you go viral. If you need help with writing a press release, you can outsource it. PRs are so short, you can get a high quality PR made for $5.

Another tip for Paid PRs: Since you are paying for each press release your publish, you better be damn sure it's perfect, because there's no going back to edit anything. Once it's on the press, it's on the press.

Oh yeah, there's also a couple different types of paid press releases you can usually buy.

One is where you pay a service to post your press release to their 1 big site, so "only the big dogs" can have their press release shown here. Another is where a service will post your press release to a larger number of press release sites (maybe 10 or 20 sites/press releases total).

If you are going to buy a press release, find the most exclusive ones, and then choose one based on your own budget. But, you want to make sure you have a small list of only the best paid press release sites.

96

Ezine/Newsletter Advertising

In my opinion, this traffic and advertising strategy is underrated. However, I think it's because it's a little more difficult to target and scale. But with new technology, these things are getting easier and better every day.

This paid traffic stratey is ezine and newsletter advertising.

Usually, ezine advertising works like this: You pay for an "ad spot" in an ezine based on the amount of subscribers that particular email list gets.

Sometimes you will pay for one ad copy in one email, and other times you will pay for an ad in a group of emails.

I find that if you use companies that tell you they can send your email ad to "millions of people" for a low cost, you usually don't get much out of it - I'll tell you about an email marketing/advertising nightmare I had in the next chapter.

If you really want some good results, you have to again find relevant content. A few chapters ago when you learned more about CPV marketing, it was best to find a relevant URL to have your ad/page show instead of. Before that, with expired domains, it was best to buy a keyworded domain that matches a keyword on your website.

With ezine and newsletter advertising, it's the same way. What do these ezines and newsletters usually send to their subscribers? Let's say for instance the "make money online niche". Even if your site and the ezine are both about "making money online", you still may not get good results if these actual people aren't interested in your website or your offer.

I find if you want to increase your visitor/investment return, you must first find the most relevant content matching your website, and then you must add so much value, that they can't possibly pass up the offer (like offering a "product" that "uuuuusually sells for $500" that is "yours now free, no restrictions"). Have a great offer, make sure you show proof that this is no B.S., and you can get some good traffic from e-zines.

97

Email List Renting

Yes, I know, in the previous chapter I said I'd tell you my nightmare of a story.

Here it goes: I was "renting" an email list (which I'll tell you about right after this story, but it's similar to the first ezine strategy) from a company that claimed they have over 100,000,000 email addresses in different niches that they can send my email ad to.

There were different prices for different packages - all were CHEAP BABY, CHEAP! I chose to go for the $50 for 1 email ad sent to 1.1 million people (yes, that's 1,100,000 people!). I thought, "Even if only 1% click on this, I'll get 11,000 website visitors! - and I could probably expect a lot more!" Then, after my email was sent to 1.1 million people, I had exactly 5 people click on the link in the email. That's a 0.0005% CTR (click through rate), which is HORRIBLE!

Lesson learned: If it's too good to be true, it probably is.

So, email list renting works like this: You are never buying and seeing any email addresses. Instead, you pay a one time fee for your email to be sent out BY the owner of the list - as if the owner was promoting your website. You never see the email addresses (although if you are subscribed to the person's list, you WILL get your email and see how it turned out). No security or data is breached. It's just like buying an ad spot, but instead it's an email being sent.

I would suggest and recommend you to rent email lists from single parties. Even if you use a website that lists a bunch of people with email lists, as long as you know the exact list and type of content that is sent to that list before purchasing, that's okay too.

You might have to pay a little more (meaning instead of $50 for 1 million sends, it's like $40 for 10,000 sends), but it's much more worth it, because it's a legitimate email list.

The problem with those big "1 million+" email lists is that they are usually created from people who either don't know or wasn't aware of what exactly they opted-in to, or from legitimate opt-ins from millions of different opt-in boxes on thousands of different websites.

There's too much randomness with these huge email lists. It's like they combine 50,000 different email lists into one to make their service sound better.

So, whether you use an email list renting directory, or if you just contact an email list owner directly, make sure your content and offer is going to be interesting to the audience it is being sent to. Quick tip: Go ahead and email the owner of the email list, and ask him about his list and your offer (let him know you are planning to rent an email from him). You can learn a lot from just asking these simple questions, and may find that an offer either will work fantastic OR isn't worth your time.

98

BUY LINKS IN POPULAR YOUTUBE VIDEOS

This is one that STILL many don't know about. But those who know about it are making bank off this strategy. You see, this strategy was started (at least in the halfway mainstream) with affiliate marketing. People would use this strategy to make money from selling products - and it worked, works, and will work for a long while (there's billions of videos haha, the list will keep going on forever!).

Alright, on to this video link buying strategy:

And yes, there are software programs out there that can automate part of this process - I've only seen this go for $1,000 or more, but if you find a cheap one, buy it - it will save you time.

First, go to YouTube and search for videos that "sort of" relate to yours. The reason I say "sort of" is because usually direct competitors won't want your website link associated with them.

When you are browsing, you are looking for the videos that have been up for a little while, and have a large amount of views (over 20,000 is preferred, you can find others with over 1 million).

Then (don't miss this part), you will check ALL of the video anyalitic statistics for each video. There is usually a button for this below the video. With this, you can see view stats for the entire life of the video. For those who privatize their stats, delete those from the list - only continue if you can see their stats.

Do some math to figure out how many views per month this video generates, and ask yourself: Is this video going to keep generating views? Do the views come consistently? How fast do the views come? - and other questions like this.

Mick Macro

Now is the tricky part: Let's say you have a music website, and you find a popular music video (on a random channel, usually uploaded by some kid) that gets an average of 50,000 new views every month. That could bring hundreds of thousands of views (and maybe millions) over the course of the next year or two.

So, you are going to buy a link in this person's video description. Send a message to the video owner stating that you'd like to pay them something like $10 or $20, and all they have to do is put your website link at the top of their video description. Since most of these video uploaders are kids, or people who don't know much about advertising, and they could use the quick money, they'll be glad to do it!

Tell them who you are, your website link, let them know this will help the both of you (you get "a little" promotion, and they get instant money). Tell them the easiest way to pay is through paypal using a "gift" money transfer. They should give you their paypal email address for payment. Then they post your link. THEN you pay them the money. Then, let them know that you have a "monitoring system", and that if they remove the link, the payment could very well be returned.

You don't want to scare them, but you do want to make it clear that no shenanigans will be tolerated. Most understand, and keep your link there forever. Also, some people will give you a counter offer and say "I'll put your link in ALL my videos for $20 more!" - and by all means, if that means you can get millions of views and link impressions, DO IT.

The thing is, this works just like any other type of advertising. You are paying for a spot to put your website link, and through the effort of choosing a great video, a low price, and getting people interested in clicking on your website link, you can expect many visitors from these YouTube videos. I will also mention one more thing: When you do this enough times, you are really creating many solid back links. And since they are on a popular YouTube video (owned by Google), Google will take notice and rank your website higher. So this strategy helps in many different ways.

99
ADVERTISE ON PEOPLE'S "THANK YOU" PAGES

This is the last traffic strategy in the book, and I wanted to leave you with something that right now, I see NO ONE doing (besides a couple of my business partners and mentors, and they love it).

This strategy is advertising on people's "thank you" pages.

What is a "thank you" page? - When someone buys a product and it leads them to a page that says "payment processed" or "thanks for ordering" or "here's your reciept", that's a thank you page. When someone opts-in to an email list, newsletter, or gets a freebie, and is led to a "you're subscribed" or "thanks for joining" page, those are thank you pages as well.

Many don't even think about advertising on thank you pages, mainly because... 1. They don't know they can, OR 2. They feel like they can get more views on their ad on the site's homepage or blog.

Here are the top reasons I love "thank you page" advertisements:

1. These people just bought something, or just joined something - or are about to receive some sort of freebie. This is the optimum time to advertise, since these people are already interested in submitting their email, downloading something, or buying something.

2. Thank you pages usually have a lot less traffic compared to the rest of their site, so you can advertise for cheap. Now, when I say cheap, it's not like it's going to be $5. For maybe a lifetime link on that page (or image link/button), or even a month or more, it could cost anywhere from $20 to $100s (don't pay any more than that).

3. Most website owners have a thank you page, but have no advertising systems set up for them. If you are going to buy an ad spot, you will usually have to email them and send them a direct payment (PayPal works, and is probably the best - any type of instant, authorized payment source). Most of these website owners won't know what to charge for an ad spot on their thank you page, since they've never done it before. This is where you come in and throw out some stats and a price they can't refuse. $20 for one month? $50 for a lifetime link? $100 for a full year?

The pricing all depends on how much you want to pay, and if the website owner is willing to accept your offer.

BONUS 1

Pocket Guide To Buying Traffic (and services to stay away from)

I just couldn't leave you without giving you a couple nice bonus guides. I hope this book and these final pocket guides help you get the traffic you want to your websites.

So, I assume after 70+ chapters of free traffic strategies, and easy instructions, you can get started with that. However, buying traffic and paid services is sometimes a more choppy wave to ride.

Buying traffic means buying actual visitors from services and websites that only claim to raise your visitor/pageview count.

Buying traffic is okay if it's from a legitimate source. All of the paid advertising techniques from this book are legitimate. So how can you tell what to go for and what to stay away from?

Well, if a website only claims they can "raise your Alexa/stat ranking", or "blast visitors to your site", and then tells you in no way should you expect interaction or any future visitors, you should stay away from them.

However, not all types of buying traffic sites are scams - some can actually be very useful. When looking for these types of sites and services, look for the ones that give a lot of details up front. Look for the ones that tell you up front that they don't use software or bots to generate views, and that the visitors are real people. It's even better if the website tells you what types of websites your traffic comes from, and how your website is being viewed.

Find a few perfect-looking websites. Then search for reviews. Listen to what other people have to say about each website or service. Look at the dates, make sure you focus mainly on the most recent reviews.

Once you find a reputable company, and you know where your traffic is coming from, what you can expect, how to get the most out of using their service (take their recommendations), and you can track everything either with your own stat system or one provided to you, you can go ahead and purchase some website traffic.

I mentioned this a few times in the book, but it's important to have a clear CTA (call to action) on the page you send this traffic to. And because you want to get return visitors, and more visitors for your money, I always recommend using an opt-in box to collect their e-mails (in exchange for a freebie, or joining a special club, or a download, or video series, e-course).

No matter what type of traffic and visitors you buy/pump to your websites, you want them to be able to see 1 clear "thing" to do. If you need more social sharing, entice people to SHARE with bookmark, social, and sharing buttons. If you want people to sign up for an e-course, email opt-in box for sure! You get the idea.

Buying traffic can seem pretty worthless, unless you are monetizing that website traffic. The next bonus guide will take you through a quick crash course to monetizing your traffic, so you can actually make some money!

BONUS 2

POCKET GUIDE TO MONETIZING YOUR WEBSITE TRAFFIC

When traffic comes, so do costs and fees. Hosting can get expensive with mass amounts of traffic. E-mail list/autoresponder "hosting" can get expensive with large amounts of e-mail subscribers.

If you know how to monetize your website and your e-mail list the right way (there's tons of right ways), you will never have any problems with getting website visitors, because you will know that even when paying for traffic, your monetization efforts are in place to make back your investment, and when perfectly monetized, will make you money.

Instead of writing a huge list of all the different monetization strategies, I'm going to give you some clear solid insight on how to monetize each of your websites correctly.

The first thing you must focus on is keeping your options open, and to never rely on any one particular monetization tactic - there's plenty of options out there.

Many newbies with just-published websites start with Google Adsense. Why? Because it's easy, and you don't have to do much. What most don't realize is that by putting all your eggs in one basket, you could lose your entire monetization strategy for your website as soon as Google says "haha, you're banned". Yes, I've been banned from Adsense, so have hundreds of thousands of others. And 99% of the time, there's nothing you can do about it.

So, first you need to get a feel for what type of monetization options are out there.

PPC Advertising (like google adsense) pays you each time someone clicks on your ad. With banner advertising, you can set a monthly payment for an ad to be shown on your site (also known as Pay Per Month ads). Affiliate marketing is when you promote someone's product with a "hop link", and get a commission when someone clicks on your link and buys the product. You could also set up and create your own products, video series, member's club, coaching program, e-book, audiobook. You could go with CPA (cost per action) ads. With these, you can get paid anywhere between 10 cents up to $10 or more for someone just entering in some information like name/email or name/email/zip code or name/email/full address, etc.

There's also Pay Per Download, where you can offer free downloads of software, and get paid $1 or $2 each time someone downloads. Can't forget physical products! Amazon has an amazing program that gives you commission on anything someone buys when you send them to Amazon.

The possibilies are endless. So when you get banned or deleted from shaky programs, just know that there are 1,000 other programs that can work even better.

I'll end this pocket guide with a few examples of what to think about when starting to monetize your site:

1. #1 - You have a website that gives away free music. You may also have a blog on that same site, as well as an e-mail list. First of all, since you give stuff away for free, you should use some "pay per download" programs, offer free downloads on your site, and get paid each time someone downloads. Next, how about some affiliate marketing? Since you give stuff away for free, you don't want to market expensive products. Start with lower priced info products that relate to your site (like making money from a music career). Then comes CPA marketing. Throw some free offers on your site, where they must click on the button, then enter their email, and you get paid $2.

   Then, think about physical products. Since people will listen to your music, put some Amazon products like headphones, speakers, music editing programs, and get paid when someone buys either those products, or ANYTHING else on Amazon. Going back to CPA marketing (I'm doing this on the fly), you could offer free downloads for a CD burner software (for people to make CDs of your music), and maybe also a free music mixing/editing program (for people to edit/mix your music). You'll get paid for each download! If you want to make money every day, put up some display/banner ads, and make money per thousand impressions, or make money per click.

2. You have a health/fitness website and blog. First, the "lose weight" and "get abs/muscle" are two evergreen niches that work great anytime. As long as you have relevant information, and many visitors coming to your site, you

can expect some great returns for affiliate products. Try some high gravity ClickBank affiliate products in the lose weight niche. If your audience is mainly women in their 40s and 50s, target some products specifically to them. Some people like reading books about fitness, so you can put some Amazon affiliate links for fitness books on your site, and even review some on your blog from time to time.

If you have lots of content on your blog, and write new articles all the time, display (CPC or CPM) ads can work great inside the content of your blog. Same goes with in-text links. This will double-underline (or dotted-underline, it's different for all companies) specific keywords on your website, and make them advertisement links, so you get paid when someone clicks on it.

3. You have an art tutorial website and blog. Affiliate marketing is great if you can find products that relate to your tutorials. Write lots of articles about photorealistic drawing, and then promote a "realistic drawing course" and get paid commissions when someone buys it. You could also promote graphic drawing tablets (like the Bamboo that is popular right now) - get an Amazon affiliate link for some drawing tablets, and post them to your site.

I would continue to focus on more affiliate programs. Art.com has an affiliate program that pays you commissions - so does DickBlick art materials. You could "brag" about the new cool art materials you got from DickBlick or Art.com, and have affiliate links (and then entice others to buy the same products). You could do video reviews for products, show the product in action - then add your affiliate link. You could create your own art book. You could sell art prints. You can promote a "sell your art" website, and get paid multiple commissions for someone you referred to join.

Bottom line...

Focus more on the audience of your site, and not just specific companies and how much money you can make.

Most people fail with affiliate marketing, because they ONLY use one company's products. Diversify your assets, and diversify your monetization strategies.

Promote some physical products from Amazon. Promote a great website (using affiliate link) from CommissionJunction. Post ads for ClickBank products. Post free CPA offers. Have dipslay and in-text advertising.

You will find that the more you diversify, the easier it is to make money. You may find that a monetization strategy that you thought was "just okay" turned out to be your #1 money maker! When you figure out what works for your specific audience, maximize your efforts with those forms of monetization.

And if you ever start to see your monetization flat-line, there's always 3 things you can do:

1. Promote more offers, and promote more often.

2. Introduce new monetization streams.

3. Get more traffic viewing your offers.

When you put everything together correctly, the sky is the limit.

Thanks For Reading!

Thanks so much for reading!

Hope you enjoyed the book, as well as the two bonus guides.

I assume you know this, but I'll say it again - In order to actually get traffic to your website, and then start making money from that traffic, you MUST be able to work hard.

At the very start (even if your website hasn't "just" started, this is still the start of your super-traffic-strategy), you must put in many hours in order to get everything set up, join websites, add content, post links, submit things, create things.

Consistency is key in online business. If you are frustrated with one traffic strategy, move on to the next one! You have plenty to choose from. You can set up all of them, and then take things one step at a time.

You don't have to do everything at once. Just make sure that each strategy you implement somehow benefits your website's traffic, branding, and monetization.

You never hear stories of people saying "I just launched my website, and somehow I get millions of visitors and make millions of dollars". It just doesn't happen. The true top dogs in the internet business that started with no money would work 15 hour days on traffic strategies like this.

But after your initial hard work, and after you've set up all of your revenue and traffic streams, you can pretty much put your online business on autopilot. But you must put in the hard work now in order to get the "magic traffic" in the future.

Where do you go from here?

First, make a list of all the traffic strategies that you know you can get started on immediately.

Then, write down what you have to do to get these started.

Start implementing these traffic strategies. Once you have all of these handled, start to introduce other strategies.

Mick Macro

Keep all of your traffic strategy info in one folder on your computer for easy viewing. Keep everything organized. You will soon have hundreds of logins, website URLs, strategies, and other info in this folder - don't make things complicated. Make things easy to find so when you need traffic, you can go and get some right away, and have a step-by-step system you can put into place now.

Now go get that traffic.

www.ingramcontent.com/pod-product-compliance
Lightning Source LLC
Chambersburg PA
CBHW051700170526
45167CB00002B/477